P9-CIV-792

THE LAST MUSTER

THE LAST MUSTER

Images of the Revolutionary War Generation

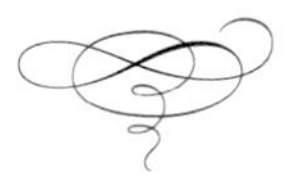

MAUREEN TAYLOR

With significant contributions by

David Allen Lambert

Library of Congress Catalog Card Number 2010000371
ISBN 978-1-60635-055-3
Manufactured in China

LIBRARY OF CONGRESS CATALOGING-IN-PUBLICATION DATA
Taylor, Maureen.
The last muster : images of the Revolutionary War generation / Maureen Taylor ; with significant contributions by David Allen Lambert.
p. cm.
Includes bibliographical references.
ISBN 978-1-60635-055-3 (hardcover : alk. paper) ∞
1. United States—History—Revolution, 1775–1783—Biography. 2. United States—History—Revolution, 1775–1783—Pictorial works. 3. United States—History—1775–1865—Biography. 4. United States—History—1775–1865—Pictorial works. 5. Portrait photography—United States—History—19th century. I. Title.
E206.T39 2010
973.3—dc22 2010000371

British Library Cataloging-in-Publication data are available.

14 13 12 11 10 5 4 3 2 1

For my dad,

James William Taylor Jr.

(1922–2007),

a member of the "Greatest Generation,"

he served with Company D

of the 389th Infantry Regiment.

CONTENTS

ACKNOWLEDGMENTS

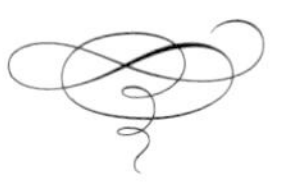

I've always been fascinated by nineteenth-century images. They let me peek into history and imagine what everyday life was like for past generations. In 1978, I saw a real daguerreotype for the first time. I was mesmerized by its appearance and the feeling that I could walk right into the scene. Since then I've worked as a photo curator, genealogist, and now as a writer focusing on photography and history.

This book recognizes that family history, photography, and American history are intertwined in the lives of the men and women pictured in these images. This work brings together all the different parts of my career—first as a history major, then as a curator working with photographs, as a librarian helping individuals find their family, and as a photo researcher/photo detective. I had to use all of the skills acquired in these roles to locate the images and to seek out the history behind them. But a project this size doesn't happen due to the efforts of one individual.

Every institution or person mentioned in the image credits made this book possible. There are many more who helped me look for pictures or searched for them on my behalf. It is too long a list to mention here, but you know who you are. Remember, you'll always have my gratitude. Unfortunately I couldn't include all the images I found due to image quality issues, or in several cases, I couldn't verify that person's place in the Revolutionary War generation due to a lack of information.

There are a few individuals who provided invaluable assistance in the production of this book. David Allen Lambert shared his collection, watched eBay for new images, and sought out facts. He contributed countless hours and valuable research to this endeavor. Erin Mulhern spent a summer as an intern helping me organize all the files and information for this project and became so indispensable that she found herself with a paying job tracking down bits and pieces of information to fill in the biographies. A friend and former colleague gave me hours of her time as a Christmas present to assist with the endless paperwork related to permissions to publish. Thank you, Jane! Craig Scott, C.G., of Heritage Books, a veteran, genealogist, and military historian, helped set me straight on all the military details. When necessary, Sheila Fuller took care of my home front activities while her husband, David, a former history teacher, proofread the manuscript.

Joanna Hildebrand Craig, my editor at Kent State University Press, believed in this project from the beginning. She coached me through the proposal process even though it took three years for me to write it while I completed book projects for other publishers. Joanna and Will Underwood (director) are extremely patient people. To encourage the completion of this long-awaited manuscript, Joanna found me an intern at the Press, Rachel Sanders. Rachel searched for last-minute images and details based on contemporary newspaper articles I found that mentioned more veterans and their widows. She kept looking despite running into more dead ends than any researcher should encounter. Thank you for keeping the faith and for your enthusiasm!

There is no single audience for the photographs and the biographies in this book. Family historians, military historians, social and cultural historians, photo historians, and anyone interested in America's past can look at these portraits and be awed by gazing at a face that knew the patriots as well as the Founding Fathers and Mothers of this country. The photographs focus on a forgotten part of American history. In each of the images you can connect with the lives of these eighteenth-century folks and by reading their vignettes get a sense of their participation in the formation of this country. The short biographies are in alphabetical order to make this book easy to browse and read in pieces. The undercurrent of the story is that each of these individuals was a real person living in a time of conflict on their home soil.

I've read and double-checked all the facts in this book, and many descendants shared their research and verified my data. Thank you for that. Any mistakes or errors that remain are mine.

Even in the mid-nineteenth century, it was difficult for historians to gather the photographs and histories of remaining Revolutionary War veterans. The records were sparse, many survivors could not write, and all parties were very old. Even a ten-year-old fifer, depending upon when he served, could have been up to eighty-five years old by 1850. The war lasted from 1775 to 1783, and over 300,000 men are said to have participated in the fight. Even if as many as 10 percent of them had portraits taken after they were commonly available in the 1840s, a lot can happen to photographs over the years. It is therefore amazing that the author could find so many portraits, and even more surprising that she could tie them to biographies, legends, and even quotes after all this time.

Maureen Taylor brings a unique combination of experience to the problem, not least being years spent as a genealogical librarian. This profession requires a special talent in the field of history, and not every graduate is drawn to this kind of demanding search for small details. Not only does the genealogist look back into family histories of births but into diaries, accounts, and portraits of past generations. And then, the study of portraits, including photographic ones, demands a knowledge of the decorative arts, fashions, and foibles of a time period, quite a separate study. This particular work was made infinitely more difficult by the fact that very old persons shunned current fashion and clung to the dress of some period in their past. Not that nineteenth-century veterans dressed in eighteenth-century clothing,

FOREWORD

Joan Severa

but at some date in their aging process they solidified their clothing choices to represent remnants of earlier lives. This is a well-documented fact in the study of nineteenth-century clothing habits. Unfortunately, there is no standard elapsed-time data, and old people dressed in anything from as much as thirty years old to perhaps ten or even five, depending on circumstances.

Because the vignettes and photographs studied here represent not only the experiences of soldiers and officers but of wives, neighbors, and children as well, the whole gives us a graphic picture of life at the time of that great conflict. War was a close and personal thing for everyone, with British and French troops marching past doors and windows (the French clomping in their wooden shoes) and camping on familiar farm fields. Mothers and wives went everywhere to nurse soldiers and sailors and encouraged their husbands and sons to join the fight for liberty. Many ten- to twelve-year-old boys went with the fathers, serving as either fifers or drummers, or simply as assistants. Families often lost multiple members in the fighting. Indian tribes fighting for the British massacred whole villages, scalping the men and killing women and children. Minutemen were summoned from farm labors to drop their tools and march immediately into battle. Sometimes their tools were the only weapons they carried into the fray.

Long and persistent research was required to gain access to the family legends and histories recounted here. Taylor is careful to point out that these stories may have been distorted by time and to give alternative interpretations where there is evidence. Yet it is the persistence of the stories that brings life to these pages. It is what makes us see the old, wrinkled visages as teenagers and young men and women, so deeply and firmly convinced of the rightness of the defense of their country that they rushed into battle against bad weather and starvation, as well as superior military strength.

Taylor's familiarity with the pension records gives us insight into the shabby and careless treatment of veterans by the government after the peace. Officers and noncoms were often the beneficiaries of land grants, but it was not until 1855 that every remaining veteran and widow could apply for land in the public domain. All were by that time extremely old and feeble. In the interim, funds were allotted or denied according to the records that were presented by applicants. In a great many cases there never were records of discharge or dates of service, and in many more they had been lost.

It is notable that Maureen Taylor has brought together here the photographs and stories of many more veterans of the Revolutionary War than were featured by nineteenth-century writers. It is a tribute to her determination and energy that this book exists. She is right: these people should not be forgotten, nor the principles for which they fought so desperately. The lesson of this book is for all of us, from the heads of government to the youngest child: when a cause is right and just, it is honorable to take it up and fight to the death, and the simplest common person who does so is a hero forever.

A portrait-history is special, too, for the demands it does (and does not) make on the viewer. While each work of history is written in a particular language and for a particular audience, here in this exhibit is a kind of history which everybody can read. It is directed to all who know the human face, what it expresses, and what it tries to conceal. "A man of fifty," Edwin M. Stanton once observed, "is responsible for his face." Everybody's face is an involuntary autobiography.

—Daniel Boorstin in *Portraits from the Americans*

INTRODUCTION

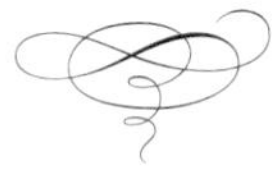

In 2002, I presented a workshop on identifying family photographs at the New England Regional Genealogical Conference on Cape Cod. As is customary with such appearances, at the conclusion of the lecture I examined objects that audience members had brought with them. One man, Jonathan Shaw, took from his pocket a cased image in pristine condition. I opened it and gasped. The interior image was clear and crisp, as if it had been taken yesterday. When I asked him if he knew anything about the man depicted, he replied, "Oh yes, that's Jonathan Leonard, my Revolutionary War ancestor who was a loyalist and spent the war in Bermuda."

It was at that moment I realized that I wanted to do this project. All the pieces of my career—historian, curator, genealogist, librarian, and photo researcher/photo detective—would come together in the pursuit of this project. I'd need my history background to understand the context of the image, the skills developed as a curator and photo researcher to locate the images, genealogical research techniques to find documentation, the photo detective identification work to understand the pictorial evidence, and the library research methods to bring all this information together throughout the process. As a former genealogical librarian, I was aware that the Census of Pensioners for 1840 contained the names of individuals collecting pensions for military service through 1840, and through my work analyzing family photographs as the Photo Detective I knew that photography was already developing in this country in 1839.[1] What if I could find more images of the Revolutionary War generation? If this man owned one, then it was very likely that there were other photo treasures like this in private and public collections. I knew of two nineteenth-century publications that featured portraits of actual veterans. In the mid-nineteenth century, Benson Lossing and the Reverend Elias Hillard retold the history of the American Revolution, Lossing in a travelogue and Hillard in a series of interviews with the survivors of the conflict.[2] Both were driven to document the rapidly disappearing physical and personal histories of the beginnings of this country. Lossing wrote in his preface, "The story of the American Revolution has been well and often told, and yet the most careless observer of the popular mind may perceive that a large proportion of our people are but little instructed in many of the essential details of that event, so important for every intelligent citizen to learn."[3] These words could have been written today, when polls show that many residents of the United States are unaware of the early history of their country, despite the fact that bookstore shelves are full of new interpretations of the Founding Fathers and Mothers and their time and place.

1. *A Census of Pensioners for Revolutionary or Military Services* (Washington, D.C.: Blair and Rives, 1841; repr., Baltimore: Genealogical Publishing, 1965).

2. Benson J. Lossing, *Pictorial Field-Book of the Revolution* (New York: Harper and Brothers, 1860), CD Heritage Books, 2004; Reverend E. B. Hillard, *The Last Men of the Revolution* (Hartford, Conn.: N. A. and R. S. Moore, 1864; repr., Barre, Mass.: Barre, 1968).

3. Lossing, *Pictorial Field-Book*, vii.

In 1848, Lossing decided to take a trip to the Revolutionary battlefields. He observed "half hidden mounds of old redoubts; the ruined walls of some stronger fortification; dilapidated buildings, neglected and decaying, wherein patriots met for shelter or in council; and living men, who had borne the musket and knapsack day after day in that conflict, occasionally passed under the eye of my casual apprehension."[4] Choosing a popular format for his presentation, Lossing decided to combine history and personal reminiscence in a travelogue of his journey revisiting past landmarks and living veterans. He intended his work partly to act as a tour guide for the younger generation and clearly stated his intention to enliven history for the average American: "As my journey was among scenes and things hallowed to the feelings of every American, I felt a hope that a record of the pilgrimage, interwoven with that of the facts of past history, would attract the attention, and win to the perusal of the chronicles of our Revolution many who could not be otherwise decoyed into the apparently arid and flowerless domains of mere history."[5] Nineteenth-century travelers could retrace his steps and read his words or take an armchair trip from the comfort of their homes. It's a romantic and colorful account of the country before the Civil War.

Lossing suggested that wartime tourism was a local phenomenon, yet travel literature suggests that this was not

4. Ibid.

5. Ibid.

the case. As early as the 1780s, foreigners came to America and commented on the remnants of Revolutionary War battlements.[6] Italian, French, and English tourists traveled throughout the states to view the landscape and the people but noted in their journals that they couldn't help but notice forts and other evidence of the war during their journeys.

Perhaps Lossing meant that in America local residents were aware of the landmarks in their area and frequently visited them. Two of the men prominent in early nineteenth-century Revolutionary War tourism are featured in this book. Nicholas Veeder of the Schenectady, New York, area converted his home into a museum of Revolutionary War memorabilia not long after the war.[7] At Fort Ticonderoga in the early- to mid-nineteenth century, Isaac Rice entertained visitors with battle stories and tours of the fort. It's interesting to note that while Lossing visited Rice, he was unaware of Veeder and his collection.

By the second decade of the nineteenth century, newspapers began publishing reminiscences of the war in conjunction with Fourth of July observances. Their correspondents paid visits to national landmarks such as Fort Ticonderoga. It is unknown when war sites began to appear as part of American travel itineraries, but it's possible that Lossing's *Pictorial Field-Book of the Revolution* became an itinerary-planning guidebook. As patriotic fervor grew with each significant anniversary of Revolutionary events, local residents honored their "last men" and held events at local landmarks. Lossing stated that he'd traveled eight thousand miles in the United States and Canada during the preparation of his work.[8] His two-volume *Pictorial Field-Book of the Revolution* became available first as installments in *Harper's New Monthly Magazine* beginning in 1850, then as a book in 1853. It's a readable firsthand account of history that is mostly lost to us today.

In 1864, the Reverend Elias B. Hillard, a Congregational minister from Connecticut aware that every newspaper mortuary notice contained the names of deceased Revolutionary War veterans, set out to photograph and interview what he thought were the final seven living veterans—Samuel Downing, Daniel Waldo, Lemuel Cook, Alexander Milliner, William Hutchings, Adam Link, and James Barham. He arrived too late to speak with Waldo and could not verify whether Barham was still alive, but each of the others entertained him with stories of their exploits during the War of Independence and the details of their everyday lives in the early years of the nation. In 1864, the House of Representatives passed a resolution increasing the pensions of the last twelve pensioners; these seven were among those

6. A list of primary accounts appears on the Fort Ticonderoga Web site, www.fort-ticonderoga.org/history/bibliographies/19th-century-tourism-fort-ticonderoga.pdf.

7. "Nicholas G. Veeder, Ex-Revolutionary Soldier," National Society of the Daughters of the American Revolution. http://members.aol.com/B1093/my-homepage/soldier.htm.

8. Lossing, *Pictorial Field-Book*, ix.

honored. Hillard described his task as an act of preservation rather than Lossing's stated educational mission, affirming, "Our own are the last eyes that will look on men who looked on Washington; our ears the last that will hear the living voices of those who heard his words. Henceforth the American Revolution will be known among men by the silent record of history alone."[9] Both Lossing's and Hillard's contributions to the historiography of the Revolution are tremendous, but both missed talking with other men who served in the United States' first military conflict. Newspaper articles in the 1850s and early 1860s regularly ran reports from the Pension Office that enumerated the men collecting pensions and their surviving wives, and then as those numbers dwindled, these features included their specific names and ages. It's estimated that close to 300,000 men served during the Revolution.

A Pension Office report published in the December 10, 1852, *New York Times* outlined the number of men and women who received support under various acts and how many were still on the rolls. The Pension Office mentioned that the total number of soldiers who received pensions under the Acts of 1818, 1828, and 1832 originally numbered more than 5,500. By 1852 there were reportedly 1,876 still on the rolls. According to that report, 6,258 Revolutionary War widows and orphans who applied under the Acts of 1836, 1838, and 1848 were still collecting in 1852. These numbers don't include those who served in the navy, individuals who received bounty or donation land, and those men who applied and were rejected.[10]

Both the Census of 1840 and this Pension Office report provide evidence that large numbers of men and women who lived during the Revolutionary War lived on into the age of photography. As a collector and former curator, I knew it was likely that images of these men and women had survived, but I also knew that many of these early images lack identification. Searching for identified images was a gamble; there was never a clear sense of how many might still survive with names intact. Given the uncertainty of this picture research, rather than focus entirely on veterans, I thought it would be wise to extend the search to widows and some significant children. This group of images would present a cross-section of the Revolutionary War generation.

After reviewing Lossing's and Hillard's work, I wondered if it was possible to use photographic and documentary evidence to re-create the first generation of Americans—those men, women, and children bound together by having lived during the Revolutionary War. I realized it was conceivable that there were pictures—daguerreotypes, ambrotypes, ferrotypes, and even paper photographs of members

9. Hillard, *Last Men,* 23. Hillard may not have been aware that, at the same time that he was writing his history, another man, G. W. Tomlinson, was compiling a list of twenty survivors. Few of those men sat for a photograph. G. W. Tomlinson, *The Patriots of the Revolution of '76: Sketches of the Survivors Etc. Etc. Etc.* (Boston: n.p., 1864).

10. Pension Office Report, *New York Times,* December 10, 1852, 6.

of that generation who lived into the age of photography. With most born in the 1760s, these hardy men and women would have been at least eighty to one hundred years of age by the time Louis Daguerre took his first daguerreotype in 1839. The focus of this project on photographs (or on paintings based on daguerreotypes) was deliberate. There are many paintings of that generation, but a photograph elicits a different response from that of viewing a painting. There is a sense of connection in a photographic portrait that extends across the centuries.

I called friend and colleague David Allen Lambert, the Online Genealogist at the New England Historic Genealogical Society. Lambert, a fellow photo collector, military historian, and genealogist, was the ideal person to ask if it were possible to locate more photographs of Revolutionary War veterans. He confirmed my suspicion and shared my excitement that there must be other images of the Revolutionary War generation out there—but where?

Tracking down the images in this volume required a multistep approach and years of research. I spoke with curators, wrote articles directed at family historians, and promoted the project to dealers and collectors. Targeted e-mails to historical societies and relevant organizations such as the Daguerreian Society helped. Results were initially mixed. A few daguerreotype collectors recalled seeing images that fit my criteria. Many times readers of my articles in the *Daughters of the American Revolution Magazine, American Spirit,* Ancestry.com, and *Family Tree Magazine* told me that no such images existed or that the only ones appeared in Hilliard's *The Last Men of the Revolution,* with which I was already familiar.[11] Fortunately, knowledgeable members of the Daguerreian Society responded with advice following an article in the *Daguerreian Society Newsletter.*[12] It didn't take long before I stopped asking for photographs of American Revolution veterans and instead began asking for images of very elderly men and women who might have been born before 1770.

Success! Images and inquiries about the project began to steadily arrive via e-mail in response to the articles. Some days I'd receive several e-mails from interested researchers and genealogists. The number of images rapidly increased from fewer than ten to nearly thirty. While there were many images in public collections or owned by collectors, I knew through my work as a curator and as a collector that there were likely even more in private family collections. To locate them I'd have to directly reach out to individuals in the genealogical community. In my role as photo detective, I give instructional lectures on identifying family photographs to historical and genealogical groups. Now each presentation included a plea for attendees to look

11. Maureen A. Taylor, "Ghosts of the Revolution," *American Spirit,* July–August 2003, 29–31; Maureen A. Taylor, "Revolutionary Pictures," *Ancestry Daily News,* November 11, 2003, www.ancestry.com/learn/library/article.aspx?article=7810; Maureen A. Taylor, "You Say You Want a Revolution," *Family Tree Magazine,* August 2003, 32–39.

12. Maureen Taylor, "Searching for the Revolutionary War Generation," *Daguerreian Society Newsletter,* July–August 2004, 8–13.

in their family collections for examples that would fit this project. I encouraged anyone in the audience who thought they owned a possible image to send me a scan in return for free research on the image to prove or disprove their claim. Whenever I mentioned this project, there was some disbelief that it was possible to locate images of these individuals. This changed once I showed some examples and described how to search their own collections. Audience members would excitedly ask me if I'd found a picture of their ancestor while others contacted me after an event with possible candidates. I'd hand out flyers at conferences so that attendees could promote the idea among other genealogists. Also, early on David Allen Lambert and I formulated a list of possible candidates to help focus the research. The 1840 Census of Pensioners contained the names and ages of men and their survivors who collected pension money for service during the American Revolution and the War of 1812, so it was easy to compile a list of individuals who were about the right age to have served in the war. Researching specific names in contemporary newspapers, local histories, and online sources yielded more names and further information. This tentative list was also helpful when asking historical societies to search their collections for the last Revolutionary War veterans and their wives in their area and when speaking with genealogical groups. Another round of articles about the project expanded my search, as did a flyer I produced to send to genealogical Web sites and blogs.

E-mails started arriving after every lecture or article publication. For instance, a descendant of Jabez Tomlinson approached me at a conference to say that his family donated their daguerreotype of him to Yale University. A Revolutionary War researcher wrote several times to suggest new places to look. By simultaneously spreading the word through print publications, advertising, talking with collectors, and searching online picture databases, more images turned up.

However, there were still hundreds more men and women listed in the Pension Records after 1839 than located photos. Where were photographs of the rest of the Revolutionary War generation? Even accounting for individuals that never sat for photographs, I knew there had to be more out there. Sitting for a daguerreotype was a novelty. By 1850 there were hundreds of daguerreotypists in the United States, and most major cities had at least one studio. The more articles I wrote, the more images were rediscovered. I wrote for genealogical magazines such as *Family Chronicle* and *Reunions,* and again wrote for Ancestry.com as well as its print publication, *Ancestry Magazine.*[13] I created a short-lived blog to promote the project, gave podcast interviews, and mentioned it in media outlets such as the *Wall Street Journal.* My Web site includes a project page with details, a

13. Maureen Taylor, "Reliving the Revolutionary War," *Reunions,* February–March 2008, 16; Maureen A. Taylor, "Clues in Military Photos," *Ancestry Magazine,* November–December 2003, 27–31; Maureen Taylor, "Revolutionary Photographs," *Family Chronicle,* January–February 2006, 40; Alexandra Alter, "The Photo Detective," *Wall Street Journal,* October 12, 2007, W1, W10.

PDF version of the *American Spirit* article, and a podcast. During my lecture trips all over the country I took side excursions to local historical societies, where curators let me browse through their photograph collections and told me about all the unidentified photographs of older people in their collections. At historical photo shows, I met with dealers, discussed the project, and handed out flyers and business cards.

After accumulating a group of pictures that represented a cross-section of the Revolutionary War population, it was clear that more were out there, but they remained either hidden in family photo collections or in private collections, or unidentified in museum and historical society collections.

The next step was to locate information about all these men and women. It was as much of a challenge as finding their portraits. The vast majority of these individuals were not wealthy, could not write, and left no written record of their life. Unlike well-known participants such as Andrew Jackson, for example, Molly Ferris Akin did not record her experiences. Instead, and as was the case with so many of the portraits collected here, her family passed down the oral tradition of her Revolutionary War heroism. I used both historical and genealogical research techniques and materials in identifying the images. Following the documentary bread crumbs of their lives meant using their portraits as historical documents. First I investigated the photo evidence, such as their clothing, props, the photographer, and any other detail present in the image. In addition to pictorial information, documents such as census records and vital records helped fill in the gaps in their personal lives. Also, printed sources such as published autobiographies, biographies, and local histories augmented the primary source documentation.

While census enumerations provided a few details, and vital records (when located) supplied background facts, it was pension records that provided insights into veterans' military service and their everyday lives, as well as vital information about their widows. In many cases documents in the files were either in their own handwriting or transcriptions of their testimony. These individuals applied for pension eligibility under a series of acts passed by Congress. These files contain descriptions of military service and depositions by friends, fellow veterans, and community leaders. The documents were often written by the applicants, offering insights into their education. An overview of the legislation provides background details about who applied when and for what benefits.

The Continental Congress passed the first pension law on August 26, 1776, offering half pay for officers and enlisted men in both land and sea units who were disabled during their service.[14] A series of resolutions meant to boost enlistment amended pension pay and offered monetary incentives for staying in for the duration of the conflict. Initially

14. Emily J. Teipe, *America's First Veterans and the Revolutionary War Pensions* (New York: Edwin Mellon Press, 2002).

there were time limits for filing applications in specific types of units. In the early nineteenth century, pension legislation made allowances for wives. There was disability or invalid pensions for those injured in the line of duty, service pensions for terms of military service, and widows' pensions for women whose husbands died during the war or who'd served a specified amount of time in specific types of units. Not everyone who applied qualified; it depended on the terms of the particular act. For instance, with the federal government feeling the financial strain of providing for all the men who qualified under the Act of 1818, the 1820 act required recipients to reapply proving their financial need. Since these 1820 pension claims usually contain an inventory of belongings and the names of individuals living in their household, it is possible to gain insights into their economic circumstances. Those veterans who did not meet the requirements were "struck from the rolls." Several of the men included in this book had their pensions revoked under this legislation. They would later have their pensions restored according to the Pension Acts of 1826 and 1828.

In all cases, men had to appear in court and show evidence of service such as either discharge papers or depositions provided by fellow soldiers. This caused a problem for most. Many men moved their families away from hometowns after the war and couldn't find individuals to support their claims, others outlived all the members of the companies, and still others could no longer find their discharge papers, if they were ever given any in the first place. Most lacked proof of their birth. Widows needed witnesses or marriage records to claim their benefits. These personal testimonies on behalf of the prospective pensioners revealed their relationships within a community, but it was also surprising just how many men and women found themselves without companionship in their later years. Pension applications include genealogical information on their families as well as a historical record of military units, battles, and actions by individual soldiers.

During the Revolutionary War, the Continental Congress also offered soldiers and their heirs land in exchange for military service. A series of resolutions passed between 1776 and 1856 outlined the terms of eligibility and specified the amount of land to which they were entitled. It ranged from 60 acres for a noncommissioned officer to 1,100 acres for a major general. In 1855 bounty land warrants (B.L.Wt.) became available from the federal government for the last time. While certain states with large territories provided veterans with land beginning in 1783, by 1793 the federal government took over the practice of doling out land in Ohio, in which military districts had been created for states with claim to the territory. The 1855 act allowed Revolutionary War veterans or their widows to apply for free land in the public domain. Each grant was for a maximum of 160 acres in areas known as the western frontier.[15]

15. Howard H. Wehmann, *Index of Revolutionary War Pension Applications in the National Archives, Bicentennial Edition* (Washington, D.C.: National Genealogical Society, 1976).

Veterans and their widows, who qualified for pensions, received varying sums distributed twice yearly. As expected, officers received more than privates. The lucky few "last men" received huge raises toward the end of their lives, granted by a Congress and a nation shamed by their prior treatment of these last living vestiges of the Revolutionary period.

As an interesting aside, during research David Allen Lambert and I estimated that a man could be no younger than sixteen for military service. We were wrong. As you'll see from reading the vignettes in this book, several of the individuals served as young children who accompanied their fathers on military campaigns. It was a surprising discovery.

In the mid-nineteenth century, Americans became obsessed with "last men." Publications featured profiles of the last dozen or so, but those lists were determined by data from the Pension office and were incomplete as far as those who actually served. Newspapers ran articles on the survivors in each state and published long obituaries for notable veterans. Given all the variables, it's difficult to pinpoint the very last man of the Revolution. Every state had one, but not all of these men sat for portraits. His image might still be out there. There are several contenders. It is easy, however, to identify the last living widow. That distinction goes to Esther Damon, who lived into the twentieth century. You'll notice that many of these "last men" died at over 100 years of age. That statistic is worthy of further study.

It has taken more than seven years to bring this book to publication. It is not a genealogy of members of the Revolutionary War, nor is it a history of the American Revolution. It is a compilation of photographs of the men and women who lived during the tumultuous formation of this country. Each portrait offers a story of their lives and of the role they played during the Revolution. Some genealogical information is given where it was pertinent to fill gaps in the historical record.

Trying to identify an unidentified photograph is a challenge. It involves a series of proofs and a set of checks and balances to sort through clues to develop a hypothesis. It takes more than a single piece of photographic evidence to put a name with a face.

Provenance—that is, the history of ownership—of an image is very important. Images in family collections, daguerreotypes, ambrotypes, and other early photographic images have often long since lost their identifications during their passage from generation to generation. However, if you can trace the trail of ownership back for several generations, then you've narrowed the possible branches of the family tree from which the image descends. Unfortunately, the vast majority of unidentified images acquired by dealers lack any background information. Even a bit of data such as the name of the estate or the previous dealer's contact information could be a lead. Photo shows are full of boxes and tables of unidentified cased, tin, and paper images.

While provenance is a key element, it's not the only piece of evidence worth investigating. There are clues in the image itself. Certain style daguerreotype mats and cases can suggest a time frame for a picture, as can styles of card photographs—thickness of the card and design, for instance. Other details such as clothing address the question of whether the sitter's attire is appropriate for the possible time period. Clothing also offers clues to religious affiliation, economic status, and occupation. A photographer's name or mark can set the image in a particular time and place. It is often possible to research those photographers to determine their work dates and city of residence.

After examining an image for details, it's time to return to ownership and family history. Family research supplies a list of possible subjects based on where the sitter lived and his/her birth and death dates. If there are identified photographs from the generation closest to the one depicted in the mystery image, then facial resemblances—shape of eyes, ears, lips, eyebrows, and faces—are also considered.

One of the most difficult aspects of an unidentified photograph is estimating age. These individuals could be old enough to be born before the Revolution, or they could be children born during or afterward.

The sum total of these facts and details can provide an answer to the questions "Who is it?" and "When was this image taken?" In the case of the images shown here, the lack of supporting evidence means they'll remain unidentified until someone recognizes them or another identified copy is located.

Unidentified couple
Collection of Paul LaFavore
Unidentified woman
Collection of David Allen Lambert

The clothing worn by the woman in the daguerreotype image suggests she is a Quaker. Her white kerchief and cap style were typical for members of that faith. The features of the man resemble those of Lemuel Cook, but without further evidence it is not possible to jump to that conclusion. The carte de visite is a copy of a daguerreotype. The edges of the original plate are visible. It's a poor quality copy with blurring of the sitter. This woman wears a shawl over her patterned dress. On her head is an old-fashioned day cap. There is no chain of ownership, no photographer's marks or name on the images. By adding up the clues that *are* apparent—clothing and style of image—it's possible to assign a tentative time frame. It's likely that both of these images were originally taken in the 1850s.

Unidentified soldier
Collection of Jeff Greene

Photography offered families a way to produce a duplicate of photographs and paintings in their collections. In the daguerreotype period, the only way to duplicate another daguerreotype was to rephotograph the original image. There were other nonphotographic duplication methods. Individuals could approach engravers to create a print version of a portrait or hire a painter to create a painted version of the original, but the only way to obtain an identical daguerreotype was to either sit for an identical image or to have a copy made. In the daguerreotype of the unknown soldier, a daguerreotypist set the painting against a surface, capturing the image, then applied color so that it became a photographic representation of the original artwork.

These short biographies represent a fraction of those Revolutionary individuals who lived into the age of photography. I'm hopeful that more images will be found. The collection covers a wide range of experiences during the Revolutionary War—from children who witnessed men enlisting, to women who stepped forward for acts of bravery, to the ordinary foot soldier who marched miles under the command of George Washington. Their images include startlingly clear daguerreotypes, paintings, engravings, and even mid-nineteenth-century paper photographs. Contemporary copies of long-lost family treasures are also included. Some paintings of the last men were not photographic but too important to leave out, as was Lossing's sketch of Isaac Rice, who supported himself giving tours of Fort Ticonderoga.

The quality of the photographic images varies widely from gorgeous, clear daguerreotypes that look like they were taken today to ambrotypes that have deteriorated to the point where the image is barely visible, such as the portrait of Mary (Seeley) Batterson. Paper prints and copy prints of earlier photographs are sometimes faded. In the nineteenth century it was common to enhance an unclear image using pencil or charcoal. This can be seen in carte de visite copy of a daguerreotype of Dr. Ezra Green; the photographer drew in eyes and wisps of hair to make them more visible. In some cases, the only images that exist of these individuals are reprints from books and are therefore less than perfect.

Each profile presents the facts of a life as collected from documents that each person left behind, be it a recitation of military service (complete with claims of glory), a newspaper obituary, or a family story. Not intended as comprehensive biographies or genealogies, they are background to the images you see: the faces of the first citizens of the United States. These portraits in picture and text allow readers to recall the Revolution through the lives of the ordinary (and some famous) individuals who were revered for their role—big or small—in the founding of the country. Some received national attention while others lived in obscurity. This is the story of the American Revolution as told through the lives of these ordinary, yet extraordinary, folks who lived through a challenging time in our country's history.

VIGNETTES

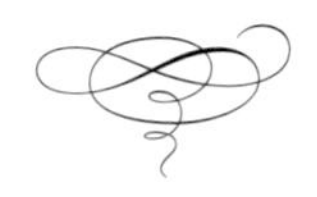

Molly Ferris Akin (April 20, 1759–October 1851)
Courtesy of Tyler Burns

Molly Ferris Akin, daughter of Reed and Annie (Tripp) Ferris and wife of John Akin, stares confidently into the camera, glasses on top of her day cap with arms crossed. It's not difficult to imagine this stoic-looking woman as a heroine. As members of the Society of Friends, also known as the Quakers, Molly and her husband, John, found themselves in a quandary during the Revolution. Quakers throughout the colonies made choices either to follow the majority of their faith and remain neutral or to take sides, risking disownment from their meeting.

At some point during the conflict Molly made a choice to help the cause. While the exact date is lost to history, family lore credits her with sneaking into a British camp near her home in Quaker Hill in Pawling, New York. Once in the camp she loaded and fired one of their muskets, thus alerting American troops to the camp's position. Afterward she crept out and returned safely to her home. While she's not as well known as other female participants, such as Molly Pitcher of the Battle of Monmouth, New Jersey, this Molly's legendary exploits have lived on in family stories passed down through the generations.

James Allen Jr. (November 24, 1768–1867)
Collections of the Maine Historical Society

On January 22, 1858, a special probate court met at Paris, Maine, to hear James Allen Jr.'s declaration of service. At "eighty nine years and upward," Allen told his life story (Pension Records). Born in New London, Connecticut, to Malachi and Abigail Allen, he recalled enlisting at Fort Griswold, Groton, Connecticut, in September 1782 as a fourteen-year-old fifer.

Fort Griswold was the site of the New London raid on September 6, 1781, that the traitorous Benedict Arnold planned as a diversionary tactic to draw allied troops away from their march to the Yorktown campaign. A square-shaped military post with fortified stone walls topped with a picket of cedar and a trench on three sides, it occupied Groton Heights, with a clear overlook of the harbor and countryside. From this spot, American troops watched as Arnold's 800 troops streamed into New London, burning everything in sight and destroying most of the town. Up at the fort, the 150 militia garrisoned there attempted to defend its arms and area but lasted only forty minutes, vastly outnumbered as they were by Arnold's forces. At the end of the battle, more than half of the Americans were dead and the rest seriously injured. As word of the outcome spread through the countryside, it's probable that Allen heard of the brave exploits at Groton and wanted to join in the action.

At his last court appearance to appeal his rejected pension application, Allen testified that he had served as a fifer at Fort Griswold from 1782 until peace was declared in 1783. He'd applied for a pension under the Acts of 1818 and 1832 and was rejected each time. In 1858 he hired an agent named Daniel Eastman of Oxford, Maine, to petition on his behalf as well as lawyers to represent him before finally appearing before the court in Paris, Maine. In 1818, Allen lacked proof of service in a Continental unit to meet the requirements of that act and in his 1858 attempt couldn't remember the names of the officers with whom he served or the identities of the other fifers. The only known witness to his enlistment still living was his younger brother, Elisha.

A deposition from Elisha, who was six at the time of his brother's enlistment and eighty-one in 1858, vaguely remembered walking his oldest brother part of the way accompanied by their mother and that he didn't see him again for two or three years. Selectmen and ministers vouched for Allen's character, but without any other witnesses to his enlistment and no discharge papers, his entire claim rested on his testimony and his brother's impassioned plea: "I have no doubt my brother served in the Army of the Revolution as he has always stated to me, and I know that he has for the last twenty years or more been trying to obtain a pension" (Pension Records).

In the 1820s Allen moved to Canton, Maine, where he found work as a carpenter. As if offering proof of his respectability, this daguerreotype shows him attired in a shawl-collared, striped dress vest with matching tie. His upturned hair is a reflection of fashion and the hat he removed for the photographer. This image likely dates from circa 1860, perhaps around the time he stood in front of Judge Thomas Brown trying one last time to prove his service. Allen died in 1867.

Ironically, Allen, who never received a pension, is known as the last Maine survivor of the Revolution.

Nathaniel Ames (April 25, 1761–1863)
State Historical Society of Wisconsin

This venerable patriot and last living Revolutionary War veteran in Wisconsin spent his later years reminiscing to crowds at Fourth of July celebrations and in front of the fire with small groups of grandchildren about his years as a soldier. Born to David and Irene (Waldo) Ames in Scituate, Rhode Island, he was raised by his grandfather, Cornelius Waldo, and in turn assisted the elder in his old age.

When his grandfather refused to let him join the service at the age of seventeen in 1779, Ames ran away to become a militia guard for a month at Fort Griswold in Stonington, Connecticut, both defending the edifice and helping to build it under the leadership of Captain Ledyard. Ledyard later lost his life at the Battle of Groton Heights during the New London raid of 1780. In June 1779 Ames enlisted in the regular army for a six-month stint at Stonington, Connecticut, serving with Colonel Betts's Company at West Point. He reenlisted in December of that year to serve as a substitute for another soldier, Joshua Barrons. Individuals were allowed to serve on behalf of another person. Discharged in 1780 at Springfield, New Jersey, having served out the remainder of Barrons's term of service, Ames then reenlisted for six months at Stonington, joining Captain Miles. He spent time at the Continental Army's winter quarters at West Point and was discharged in January 1781. Ames recalled these basic facts for his pension application of 1833 and received an annual sum, despite having lost all his discharge papers and having no witnesses to his service. He also testified that he hadn't been in any battles but had been present at the hanging of the British spy, Maj. John André, a compatriot of the traitorous Benedict Arnold.

For the remainder of the conflict, Ames served on a New London–built sixteen-gun privateer brig, the *La Fayette*. He sailed to Newport at the same time that a French fleet arrived in the harbor. He recalled waking to noise on the sidewalk outside his room caused by the wooden shoes worn by the French troops. Ames witnessed Gen. George Washington's celebratory arrival in Newport. These events probably took place in 1779. In the summer of 1778, the Americans with French assistance tried to rout the British from Newport and failed. The city was a strategic location for the British, who wanted access to New York City, and the redcoats captured the town and held it until they abandoned it in 1779. The French, under the command of Rochambeau, then arrived in the city, and the townspeople welcomed George Washington.

At war's end Ames joined the crew of another ship. He contracted a near-fatal case of yellow fever before returning home to Connecticut. After the war, Ames's father lost all his property in Connecticut due to the devaluation of the colonial currency and moved to Vermont, but his son chose to move west. Ames first settled in a series of New York towns—Waterford, Coeymans, and Steuben—before moving to Racine, Wisconsin, and then to Dane County. He married Sarah Hall in 1789 and had eleven children, ten of whom lived into old age. Ames died at the age of 102 years 4 months 2 days.

On his 102nd birthday, Ames's grandson with whom he was living gave him a party complete with band. Ames then entertained the guests with his wartime memories, including stories of the treason of Benedict Arnold and the execution of Major André. Not long before his death, when asked about the war, he recalled meeting Washington and General Baron von Steuben. He began to cry and asked attendees for their forgiveness for his emotional response: "You must excuse these expressions of an old man's weakness, for I can never think of those good men without causing my heart to be stirred within me" (*Wisconsin Patriot*).

Hundreds of people attended his burial service, including representatives from all the Masonic lodges in the area. Ames had been a Mason for sixty-five years. Upon his death his grandson (name unknown) wrote a sketch of his life for the *Wisconsin Daily Patriot* that ended, "Permit me to add Grandfather Ames died as he had lived[,] an unflinching Democrat."

Wisconsin artist Samuel Marsden Brookes painted this portrait of Ames at ninety-nine years of age. In the portrait, Ames gazes directly at the artist, a self-confident man secure in his beliefs. In February 1859, Brookes sold his work to the Wisconsin Historical Society for fifty dollars.

George Avery (January 23, 1759–January 31, 1857)
Avery Genealogy

George Avery stares at the camera with steady eyes and a serious expression in this portrait. Born in Truro, Massachusetts, to Job and Jean (Thatcher) Avery, he enlisted at the age of sixteen in Captain Sellew's Company, helping to guard the coast against British vessels. At the conclusion of his service in 1779, he moved to Windsor, Connecticut, and reenlisted for one month in Capt. Benjamin Allen's Company during the winter of 1780. By August of that year, he was in Sharon, Vermont, and present for the burning of the newly chartered town of Royalton by Native Americans.

Zadock Steele, one of the survivors of the incident at Royalton, wrote a memoir of the events of October 16, 1780, published in 1818. He remembered that three hundred Indians from various tribes came to town from Canada under the command of a British officer and a Frenchman. Although their original target was the nearby town of Newbury, they instead destroyed Royalton, scalping men, killing women, plundering goods, and burning homes. In 1845, Avery gave an account of his own experience that appeared in the 1893 *Genealogical Record of the Dedham Branch of the Avery Family,* with some confusion as to the date. "It occurred at about the same time in the month of September 1782—now 63 years ago—and I feel yet these emotions and cannot help the tears gushing from mine eyes."

He described his youthful demeanor as "a giddy youth with vain expectations to be something in the world" (*Avery Family,* 322). He recalled traveling with a careless group of comrades, not following the Sabbath, and on occasion offering rude comments in contradiction to his upbringing. All that changed in a single day.

While he went to fetch bread from a neighbor and his friends prepared breakfast, a group of Indians approached them. Unlike his companion, Avery initially didn't feel threatened. When confronted by two members of the invaders, one bearing a tomahawk, he fled, only to be followed. After he was struck in the back with a tomahawk and found himself unable to walk after repeated blows from the weapon, the Indians removed his coat and took him prisoner. They forced him to accompany them to an area where tribal members burned buildings and took others prisoner. That night, October 16, 1780, he counted 350 Indians and 26 prisoners.

As several prisoners were led out of sight by Indians, a fellow prisoner remarked that he thought they were going to be killed. Avery believed that the Indians meant to kill him when he was staked to the ground with his feet to the fire. When the Vermont militia came close to the camp, Avery's belt was placed around his neck, and he was led by this noose until they reached St. John's Canada. Dressed like an Indian with face paint and wampum, Avery and one other prisoner were admitted to the tribe to replace two men who had died. The rest of the prisoners were killed and their scalps displayed in a tribal ceremony. Six weeks later he was in Montreal being traded for bounty. He'd remain in British captivity for twenty months.

Avery described this whole experience as a turning point in his life. "I felt the evil of my life and the Divine Justice of Providence" (*Avery Family*, 325). After his release in Whitehall, New York, Avery walked first to his sister's house in Windsor, Connecticut, and later to visit his parents in Truro, reassuring everyone that the reports of his death two years earlier had been false.

Seven years after he was freed from being a prisoner of war, he married Mary Sanborn of Hawke (Danville, New Hampshire) on January 11, 1789. They had twelve children together. Avery received a pension for his Revolutionary War service from 1834 until his death on January 21, 1857, and his invalid wife, Mary, collected widow's benefits for seven more years.

When he applied for a pension under the Act of 1832, the War Department disputed his claim. In response, Avery hired an agent who located two fellow captives named Garner Rix and Phinias Parkhurst. Both came forward to substantiate Avery's claim of captivity, but neither could vouch for his Revolutionary War service. Avery received a pension in 1834 with payments retroactive to September 1831. He received a pension continuously from that point until his death in 1857. Upon his death, his widow applied for and received a pension.

At the end of his life, it was family, faith, and Republican principles that mattered most. His obituary claimed that he had voted in every election. His direct gaze and stern expression in this photograph reflect his religious conviction and character.

Anna Warner Bailey (October 11, 1758–January 19, 1851)
Monument House Museum at Fort Griswold

Anna Warner Bailey, daughter, wife, and mother, became known as a local heroine for her part in the American Revolution as well as a national celebrity for her actions during the War of 1812.

In the former conflict, she was reportedly the first woman to arrive at Fort Griswold, Groton, Connecticut after the battle that took place on September 6, 1781. She found her uncle mortally wounded and discovered her future husband, Elijah Bailey, a prisoner of the British. At her uncle's request, she returned home to gather his family so that he could see them again before dying. Two years later, in 1783, she married Bailey, and together they operated a popular tavern in town.

In July 1813 a fleet of British ships entered New London harbor, and residents, fearing an invasion, moved their women away from the coast, and the Connecticut militia again kept watch at Fort Griswold. Ill-prepared for an armed conflict, the soldiers needed supplies, among them flannel for gun wadding and ammunition. In 1847, the *Morning News* recounted the day's events as told by the messenger arriving in town from the fort. Bailey and another person gathered what supplies they could from remaining citizens, but when that proved to be inadequate, "Mrs. Bailey, was not to be defeated in her object. She instantly *threw off her petticoat from her own person, where she stood in the street,* exclaiming, as she gave it to him, 'There, put that in the d——Englishmen's g——ts!" This one action catapulted her to regional and then national fame.

In later life in her hometown of Groton, Bailey was known for her passionate support of the United States and her strong feelings about Benedict Arnold's traitorous act. The town honored her by making her postmaster for life. She died at the age of ninety-three when her clothes caught fire while she napped near an open fireplace.

In 1896, Frances Lester Roland wrote a memorial poem in recognition of her character and appearance for the *Daughters of the American Revolution Magazine:*

> Mistress Anna Warner Bailey.
> As a maiden she was comely,
> Bright blue eyes and golden tresses,
> She, the belle of all the country.

While not honored on the monument to the men who fought at Fort Griswold during the American Revolution, the Anna Warner Bailey Chapter of the Daughters of the American Revolution have use of the stone house adjacent to it. Two paintings and a photographic portrait reported to be Bailey hang in the house in her memory. In the one pictured here, she wears a day cap on her head. For this to be Bailey it would have been based on a daguerreotype taken prior to her death in 1851.

DANIEL FREDERICK BAKEMAN,
The last Revolutionary Soldier, one hundred and nine years old.
Entered according to act of Congress, in the year 1868, by A. D. CROSS, in the Clerk's Office in the District Court of Mass.

Daniel Frederick Bakeman (October 10, 1759–April 5, 1869)
Collection of the author

In nearly every colonial state there is a "last man" of the Revolution, but the honor of being the very last living soldier of that conflict is in dispute. It's likely that Daniel Frederick Bakeman holds the distinction of being the longest living pensioner, but there are other claimants to being the last living soldier. In the 1860s, with political tensions building into what would become the Civil War, many were interested in documenting the history of these last men. At the time that Rev. Elias Hillard traveled the country interviewing seven survivors for his book *The Last Men of the Revolution,* Bakeman was not included. It's likely that Hillard never heard of Bakeman, who only received a pension on February 14, 1867, through a special grant of the U.S. Congress because he lacked proof of service. He claimed four years of service from 1779 to 1783 beginning in Capt. William Van Arnum's Company. He received five hundred dollars annually retroactive to July 1, 1866.

This carte de visite commemorates the occasion of Bakeman's being named the "the last Revolutionary soldier" and was likely sold as a collectible image. Carte de visite images were first introduced in the United States in 1859. A caption below reads, "The Last Revolutionary Soldier, one hundred and nine years old." It was registered in Massachusetts in 1868 by A. D. Cross. It's a photograph of a heavily enhanced image of Bakeman.

Bakeman died two years later at an advanced age. Newspaper accounts mention his age as 109 or 111, but perhaps he knew best: in his pension claim before a justice of the peace in 1867 he claimed to be 107. A sketch of his life written in the *Duluth News Tribune* in 1903 claims his birth year as 1759, that Susan Brewer became his wife when she was 24 and he 22, and that they had eight children.

This legendary couple was well known in their town of Freedom, New York, and after Bakeman received a pension they became local celebrities, participating annually in Fourth of July parades. It's said that he never missed an opportunity to express his loyalty by shooting his Revolutionary War musket, which he called his "Howling piece" (*Duluth News Tribune*). Supposedly he'd raise it over his head using both arms, shouting, "Hurrah for Washington, Putnam, and Lee, and all the brave sons who fought for liberty."

Amos Baker (April 8, 1756–July 16, 1850)
Courtesy of the Concord Public Library

In this crayon portrait that combines artistic rendering and photography, Amos Baker's distinguished visage suits the man credited with being the last living soldier of the fight at the North Bridge, as part of the Battle of Lexington and Concord, April 19, 1775. It is likely based on a daguerreotype, the location of which is currently unknown.

A Lincoln, Massachusetts, native, Baker was born on April 8, 1756. In his pension claim of 1833, he related in court his military service. Baker enlisted formally in December 1776 in a militia company under the command of Moses Harrington for four months, which he spent at Dorchester, Massachusetts. In November 1777, he served an additional five months. For proof of service he supplied discharge papers and three credible witnesses.

He lived into his ninety-fourth year, long enough to be a participant in the seventy-fifth anniversary of the Battle of Lexington and Concord on April 19, 1850, held in Concord. According to the *Boston Daily Evening Transcript,* only four other Revolutionary War veterans were there: Jonathan Harrington and Abijah Harrington of Lexington, Dr. Preston of Lincoln, and Thomas Hill of Charlestown. Baker was thought to be too infirm to speak about his service during the battle but remarked, "I really believe I felt better all that day, taking it altogether, than I should have felt had I staid at home" (*Boston Daily Evening Transcript*).

Three days later Baker was in court providing an affidavit in vindication of another soldier, Capt. Isaac David of Acton, who was seeking his share of the honors of the battle. It's a remarkable account of the events. Baker was nineteen years old on that April day; also in his brigade were his brothers, Nathaniel, James, Jacob, and Samuel, as well as his brother-in-law Daniel Hosmer. The captain of the brigade, Col. Abijah Pierce, came armed with a cane until he took a gun from a dead British soldier. One of Baker's companions, Noah Parkhurst, remarked, "Now the war has begun and no one knows when it will end" (*Letter to Lemuel Shattuck*). Baker also remembered that he was the only soldier in that fight with a bayonet, because his father had gotten it in the French war, a reference to the French and Indian War. He was unable to verify that David had been in the fight.

In July 1850 attorney Josiah Adams went to Baker's house to question him further but found him so frail that he doubted his recall of events. Baker died on July 16, 1850.

Mary (Seeley) Batterson (c. 1763–1858)
Private collection

This ambrotype probably depicts widow Mary (Seeley) Batterson as she looked in the late 1850s, not long before her death. The seventeen-year-old Weston, Connecticut, resident married Revolutionary War veteran George Batterson on May 11, 1779. They had twelve children.

Her husband applied for a pension in 1818 for his service in the Continentals, in Capt. Joseph Allyn Wright's Company, Col. Heman Swift's Regiment, in the 2nd Connecticut as of February 4, 1781. Batterson was discharged in December 1783, at New York, after the British left the area.

Family lore relates, "At the time of the attack of Fairfield, Connecticut, his mother had just removed a piece of cloth [from the loom] she had woven with her own hands and George hid it in the hollow of a sycamore tree. After the danger had passed he recovered the cloth from which she made him a suit of clothes, which he wore as a soldier in the patriot army" (Cutter, *Genealogical and Family History of the State of Connecticut,* vol. 3, 1239). The occupation and burning of Fairfield occurred on July 8, 1779.

In 1820, Batterson reapplied for a pension and showed need of continued support. Included in his pension claim was the required inventory of the couple's belongings to prove their financial straits—total value $57.84. He specified one house (on the highway), valued at $30; one cow, $20; a loom, $5; a brass kettle, $1.50; an iron pot, $1.75; six tea cups and saucers, $1.25; three forks and knives, $1.25; and two white bowls, $1.10.

After his death in May 1837, Mary appeared in court to apply for widow's benefits, recounting her husband's service details and stating where and when they married. She began receiving a widow's pension of eighty dollars annually. In 1855 she applied for and received bounty land under the Act of 1855.

The deterioration of the backing on this image distorts the details of Batterson's dress, but thankfully not her face. From beneath her day cap she peers directly into the photographer's lens, which captures her aged condition. At the time of her death she lived with her daughter Anna and her daughter's husband, Frederick R. Smith. She lived to be ninety-five.

Jesse Betts (August 27, 1764–August 1, 1854)
Hannah (Paxson) Betts (February 19, 1766–March 3, 1852)
Private collection

This lovely pair of daguerreotypes was taken by the couple's grandson, Benjamin Betts (1822–1908) who studied with the well-known daguerreotypist Samuel Broadbent in Wilmington, Delaware. Betts took over Broadbent's studio in 1851, beginning a partnership called Betts and Carlisle. Their specialty was stereoscopic daguerreotypes from life. Betts left the firm in 1854 to move to Philadelphia. It is unknown who painted these daguerreotypes, but it was likely one of the artists Betts associated with in Wilmington.

Jesse Betts, son of Zachariah and Rachael (Bye) Betts, was born in Bristol Township in Bucks County, Pennsylvania. His wife, Hannah Paxson, was born in Solebury Township in the same county. The couple married September 19, 1787, and had five children. Jesse Betts worked as a carpenter. Both Solebury and Bristol townships were settled primarily by Quaker families, with Bucks County being one of the original areas inhabited by followers of William Penn. Their attire in these daguerreotypes reflects their religious beliefs. Quakers dressed in a plain manner, without adornment. Hannah wears a simple shawl and day cap while her husband wears a collarless vest, jacket, and tie.

As members of the Society of Friends, and pacifists, it's likely they abstained from military service during the American Revolution. In September 1776, the Philadelphia Yearly Meeting advised its members to remain neutral, asking them not to participate in any action that could be viewed as taking sides such as voting, loyalty oaths, military service (even obtaining a substitute to serve in their stead), and paying taxes. The result was that Quakers were persecuted by both sides—by Americans (for being loyalists) and by the British (for being patriots). Neither side trusted their neutrality. It's unknown what type of persecution the Bettses experienced during the war.

After the Revolution, the couple stayed in Pennsylvania until they moved to Delaware, where their son Mahlon lived. He was a prominent machinist and industrialist in the Wilmington area.

In the 1850 Federal Census, the couple was living in Wilmington, Delaware, another city with a large Quaker population. At that time Jesse was eighty-six years old and listed as the head of household. His occupation was a pattern maker (someone who makes wood patterns for metal objects). He lived with his eighty-four-year-old wife, Hannah, their sixty-two-year-old daughter, Rachel, and an Irish maid, aged twelve. It is probable that they sat for these portraits in the early 1850s, when their grandson began his career as a daguerreotypist and not long before they died.

Josiah Brown (October 1, 1766–January 20, 1858)
Bennington Museum, Bennington, Vermont

A handwritten note inside this daguerreotype identifies him as "Josiah Brown[,] Grandma Winslow's Grandfather[,] Aged 91 yrs. when the picture was taken." If that note is factual, then this image was taken in 1858 shortly before Brown's death.

Born in New Ipswich, New Hampshire, he was the eldest son of Capt. Josiah Brown and Sarah Wright. He married Millicent Wright, daughter of Edward and Thankful Wright, on April 19, 1792. Three years later they, along with five of his brothers and one sister, moved to Whitingham, Vermont. The couple had nine children, but only four lived into adulthood.

His father, Captain Brown, served in the American Revolution, fighting at the Battle of Bunker Hill. The *History of Whitingham* (1886) relates a story told by Captain Brown about one of the men in his regiment at the battle: "After we had orders to retreat, a brave youth of seventeen, who had fought by my side all day, had just loaded his musket and was returning his ramrod to its place, when a British Officer rode up flourishing his sword, not ten feet distant, exclaimed 'My boy, lay down your arms, we've won the day.' The young brave, nothing terrified drew up his gun and shot the officer down, and retorted, "[']There G—— d—— you you've lost it,['] and turned and run amidst a shower of bullets, and escaped unharmed." His son Josiah never enlisted in this conflict.

In this picture, a serious looking Brown with a furrowed brow focuses his light-colored eyes on the photographer. In one hand he holds a pair of spectacles and in the other, a book. As both Josiah and his wife, Millicent, were founding members of the Baptist Church in Whitingham, this could be a Bible or perhaps a ledger. He eventually served a one-year term as town clerk. As an aged man, he moved to Bennington to live with his son Edmund.

Caesar (1737–1852)
Collection of the New-York Historical Society

According to the caption on the back of this daguerreotype, four generations of a New York family owned this man, reputed to be the last slave to die in the North. This label supplies all the information known about his life.

Born as a slave in 1737 in Bethlehem, New York, his first owner was William Nicoll's son, Van R. (probably Rensselaer), who after his death at age seventy on August 5, 1776, willed the thirty-nine-year-old Caesar to his son, Francis. Col. Francis Nicoll (1737–1817) participated in the American Revolution. Upon his death on September 14, 1817, at the age of seventy-nine, the then octogenarian Caesar became the property of Francis's grandson, William Nicoll Sill (1786–1844) until William's death on March 17, 1844, at the age of fifty-eight years. William left his estate, along with the care of the 107-year-old Caesar, to his wife, Margaret (Mather) Sill.

In the Dutch colony of New York, slaves could be members of the Dutch Reformed Church and thus baptized at birth and married in a religious ceremony. The Dutch allowed them to testify in court, enter into legal agreements, and file civil suits. They even permitted their slaves to earn "half-freedom" to live separately in their own community and pay taxes. In 1664, the Dutch West India Company freed some of its slaves, allowing others to purchase their freedom. Many private families retained their slaves. Any new slaves imported into English New York remained slaves for life as an inherited estate; even their descendants were forced to became slaves. It's estimated that 40 percent of New York families owned slaves.

In 1741, a few years after Caesar's birth, New York City was the scene of a slave uprising. Known as the "Great Negro Plot," blacks burned buildings and created general mayhem in the aftermath. Thirty blacks were executed as a result of the burnings.

During the American Revolution the British promised freedom to any slave who served on their side. After the war, they transported to Canada more than three thousand slaves who had supported their cause. New York residents who believed in the tenets of the Revolution began to question slaveholding policies. Not everyone agreed, but a series of gradual emancipation laws was passed. By 1790, New York still had more slaves than any other northern colony. Slavery finally ended in New York in 1827.

While legally a free man, Caesar could have left the family, but at the advanced age of ninety, he continued to live in the house in which he was born to work for the family that had owned him for close to a century. He would remain in their employ until his death at the age of 115 in 1852.

According to a register of stones in the Nicoll-Sill cemetery in Bethlehem, somewhere on the property is a grave for "Old Caesar," who spent his life in service at the Nicoll-Sill house, now known as the Bethlehem House.

Caesar lived his entire life as a house slave passed from house owner to house owner. Rensselaer Nicoll built his mansion in 1735, willed it to his son, Francis, who then gave it to his grandson, William, who lived with him as a child. Caesar's final owner, Margaret (Mayer) Sill, outlived him, dying at the age of seventy-seven on May 1, 1866.

In this daguerreotype taken in 1851, the 114-year-old Caesar looks spry for a man of his age. Dressed in a plaid vest with walking stick in hand, he shows no evidence of infirmity in his gaze or countenance.

Noah Callender (February 28, 1768–August 19, 1851)
Vermont Historical Society

On May 10, 1775, when Amos Callender and the rest of Ethan Allen's Green Mountain Boys decided to attack Ticonderoga and retrieve the arms stored there, Callender's seven-year-old son, Noah, accompanied his father.

The major officers of this attack were Ethan Allen and Benedict Arnold. Although Allen had been given command of the action, Arnold disputed the claim, jeopardizing the success of the operation. In an address before the Vermont Historical Society in 1872, Louis Chittenden recounted Noah Callender's memories of the conflict between the two men. It is a secondhand account as remembered by a child, but Callender was considered a credible source by his peers. Reportedly, when Allen gave the command to attack, Arnold claimed that he had the right to lead the charge and enter the fort first. An argument ensued, and Allen asked Amos Callender, "What shall I do with the d——d rascal? Shall I put him under guard?" Callender advised Allen to settle the dispute by attacking side by side. Both men agreed. Allen later confirmed these events in his *Narrative of Colonel Ethan Allen's Captivity* (1779). Allen was considered a hero, whereas four years later Arnold became infamous as a traitor who offered his services to the British.

Noah Callender later married Sarah Smith, daughter of John and Sarah (Doolittle) Smith, in 1794. They had two children. He died at the age of eighty-three. In this daguerreotype, the well-dressed Callender in coat and wrapped silk tie looks uncertain about the photographic process.

Ezra Carpenter (March 25, 1752–July 1, 1841)
Courtesy of Laura G. Prescott

As an elderly man, Ezra Carpenter would gather his grandsons to tell them about his role in the American Revolution. It's a tale he recounted whenever he had the chance. His story appeared in the *Carpenter Memorial,* a genealogy of the family.

"About four o'clock in the afternoon of the 21st [of April 1775] the news of the battle reached Foxboro [Massachusetts] with the call to the 'minute-men' to march at once to the assistance of the American troops near Boston. Ezra was in the field ditching when he received the news; leaving his spade in the ditch he hastened home and with his stepmother's assistance packed his knapsack and at sunset on that April night, started on foot for the seat of war." Carpenter remembered walking as far as Walpole, where he rested for the night but didn't sleep. He recalled, "I was so excited and anxious to fight the red-coats." He met up with his regiment in Dedham and spent two days marching to Boston. In later years he regretted being only a witness and not a participant at the Battle of Bunker Hill. He was close enough to the action, however, that a "stray bullet cut his underclothing[,] grazing the skin[,] and killed a cow."

In 1830, the seventy-seven-year-old Ezra appeared in court to appeal his case to receive a pension under the Acts of 1818 and 1820. He mentioned formally enlisting on April 24, 1775, just days after the first shots at Lexington and Concord. He served as a private for eight months under the command of Capt. Oliver Pond in Col. Joseph Read's Massachusetts Regiment. Carpenter ended up serving several tours of duty and was present at the Battle of Princeton and Trenton, New Jersey, in 1776.

Although his name appeared on the pension rolls of 1818, he was dropped from the list in 1820 because he owned property. In 1830, in debt and ill with rheumatism, he reapplied for a pension, telling the pension office he sold his land to his son Ezra in 1824 but lacked written documents to confirm the transaction. Carpenter also stated that he had no income to support himself and his wife, being totally dependent on family. A year later his agent and attorney, Benjamin Cowell, wrote a letter to the pension office in outrage at Carpenter's removal from the rolls. "There was no question as to his revolutionary services. There was no question as to his poverty, nor can there be in the minds of anyone—to that fact he produced the testimony of his neighbors, and if I remember right the testimony of the Select men, of the town indeed no one, in the community who knows the man doubted his pretensions in any respect to a pension—Under the circumstances of this case I ask if the Rules of the pension office can be allowed to interfere with the administration of Justice? . . . I ask, which is to take precedence, the laws of the land or arbitrary rules?" (Pension File). Carpenter was awarded an annual payment of $74.64. When he died in 1841, his second wife, Mary/Polly Daniels, returned to the court to verify that she was his widow, having married him on December 16, 1790.

The original picture of Carpenter was a daguerreotype taken just before his death in 1841, which was then later copied and enhanced using artistic techniques to fill in the details. The photographer/artist didn't accurately copy the knobs on the back of the chair (still owned by the family), and it's possible he enhanced other details as well. In this late nineteenth-century photographic copy of the rendering, Carpenter poses in his favorite chair, hands clasped, with long hair. The chair remains in the family, along with the portrait.

Family tradition holds that as Ezra's rheumatism worsened and he became more stooped, the legs of his chair were sawed off so that he could rise more easily. His posture in this image clearly shows that the lowered chair legs made him slump when seated.

Chainbreaker, also known as Governor Blacksnake and Tah-won-ne-ahs (c. 1749 or c. 1760–December 18, 1859)
Extra Census Bulletin: Indians; The Six Nations of New York

This Seneca chief who fought for the British during the American Revolution first dictated his memoir to a neighbor and fellow Seneca, Benjamin Williams, at Cold Spring, New York, during the winter of 1845–46. Williams then wrote it down in English. There is no record of Chainbreaker's exact date of birth, but it could be as early as 1749.

In his reminiscences, Chainbreaker recalled that in January 1776 a meeting took place at a convention held at Pittsburgh. A group of patriots asked the representatives of the Six Indian Nations to remain neutral in the conflict. Tribal leaders responded by leaving it up to their tribal members. The Seneca people sided with the Iroquois chief, Joseph Brandt, who fought for the British. Chainbreaker acted in the capacity of a soldier from 1777–83 and told how he was present at the Battle of Oriskany (New York), when the Indians and British ambushed American troops. In retaliation, the American major general John Sullivan burned their villages and crops. After the war, Chainbreaker lived on the Allegheny Reservation in Cattaraugus County, New York, and fought for the United States during the War of 1812. He died on the reservation in 1859.

Shortly before his death, he posed for this daguerreotype. The location of the original is currently unknown, but it was reproduced in Thomas Donaldson's *Indians—The Six Nations of New York: Cayugas, Mohawks (St. Regis), Oneidas, Onondagas, Senecas, Tuscaroras,* published in 1892. An 1845 painting by John Phillips is in the Rochester Museum and Science Center Collections.

Lemuel Cook (c. 1764–May 20, 1866)
Reverend E. B. Hillard, The Last Men of the Revolution

When the Reverend Elias Hillard interviewed and photographed Cook, the veteran claimed to be 105 years of age and was at that time thought to be the oldest survivor of the American Revolution. His actual date of birth is unknown, although an obituary in the Washington, D.C., *Daily Constitutional Union* listed his age as 102 in 1866. Cook reported to Hillard that he was born in Plymouth, Litchfield County, Connecticut, in 1764.

According to Cook, he first enlisted in 1781 when he was sixteen. "When I applied to enlist, Captain Hallibud told me I was so small he couldn't take me unless I would enlist for the War" (Hillard, *Last Men,* 61). He enlisted to serve in Col. Elisha Sheldon's Second Regiment of Light Dragoons out of Northhampton, Massachusetts. Light dragoons rode into battle but dismounted to fight as infantrymen. Cook mustered into Capt. William Stanton's unit of infantry. He also told Hillard he nearly died while on sentry duty at Dobbs Ferry, New York, when a British soldier fired and the musket ball hit his hat. During this skirmish he met French soldiers for the first time and was impressed with their way of marching and their manner, stating that he thought they were a "proud nation."

Cook received one hundred acres for his service until the end of the war under the provisions of the Continental Congress resolution of September 16, 1776. He first received a pension in 1818. Under the land act of 1855, Cook received an additional sixty acres. As of 1865 his pension was five hundred dollars a year.

During Hillard's interview, Cook recalled being at the Battle of Brandywine, present at Cornwallis's surrender at Yorktown, and that Baron von Steuben selected him to come along on the New York City campaign. Hillard described Cook's demeanor: "He recalls the past slowly, and with difficultly but when he has fixed his mind upon it, all seems to come up clear." Cook could no longer recall all the events in which he participated, and he became confused at times.

At the conclusion of the war, Cook married and then moved to Utica, New York. Each veteran Hillard interviewed commented on the Civil War, but Cook's response was especially passionate: "It is terrible; but, terrible as it is, the rebellion must be put down!"

Samuel Curtis (July 30, 1779–August 25, 1879)
Collection of the author

This photograph was unidentified until recently. Based on the photographer's imprint, date on the back, and research in published vital records, it was determined that this was a picture of centenarian Samuel Curtis. His obituary in the *Boston Daily Advertiser,* August 25, 1879, mentioned this picture:

> *A Centenarian's Death*
> Mr. Samuel Curtis died at Marshfield on Thursday, the 21st instant, at the age of one hundred years and three weeks. On the day which rounded out his full hundred years all his living descendants gathered at his house and there was a joyous celebration. He was then in his usual health, and the morning after rose at five o'clock to give the parting word to guests who stayed with him over night. A week before his death he suffered a slight paralytic shock, such as he had experienced before, but this time his advanced years made him too weak to rally. He was born in the house in which he died, and had lived quietly as a farmer all his life. On his last birthday he had his photograph taken twice, once alone and once in a group.

Curtis, son of Samuel and Mary/Mercy Jayce, was born during the American Revolution on July 30, 1779, in Marshfield, Massachusetts. Curtis probably spent his childhood hearing stories of his father's military exploits. His father, Samuel, served as a private with Capt. William Turner's band of minutemen, which referred to a select group of men who could be ready to fight in under a minute. Turner's men answered the call for troops during the Battle of Lexington and Concord, April 19, 1775.

This photograph is likely the single portrait taken on his one hundredth birthday. He's seated in an upholstered chair. In the background is a papered wall and a piece of furniture. The location of the group portrait is unknown.

George Washington Parke Custis (April 30, 1781–October 10, 1857)
Library of Congress

In 1845, fifty years after his last visit to New York, George Washington Parke Custis returned to the city while on a tour of Revolutionary War sites. As the grandson of Martha Washington and the adopted son of George Washington, his visit was a cause for celebration. Newspapers carried the story that, in August 1845, there was a reception for him attended by "the friends and companions in arms of the great Washington." According to contemporary accounts, there "were veterans who had fought in the revolution, and who, despite modern customs[,] still adhere to the old style of dress—the broad skirted coat, breeches, low shoes and white silk stockings. Here were officers of whom history makes honorable mention—gentlemen who, though sojourning among us with the bleachings of many winters upon their heads, are still hale, hearty, vigorous and light-hearted."

Custis was the son of John Parke Custis (the only son of Martha Washington and her first husband) and Eleanor Calvert. He came to live with the Washingtons when his father died of camp fever in 1781, leaving four children fatherless, including the six-month-old George. Washington quickly adopted the two youngest children so that Martha could help care for her grandchildren. Spoiled by his grandmother and disciplined by an absent adopted father during his childhood, Custis's character was examined by his daughter after his death: "While the public duties of the Veteran [Washington] prevented the exercise of his influence in forming the character of the boy, too softly nurtured under his roof, and gifted with talents which, under a sterner discipline, might have made him more available for his own and his country's good" (Moore, *Family Life of George Washington,* 149).

When Custis was twenty-one, he inherited his biological father's estate, his grandmother's land, and parcels of land around Mount Vernon from his adoptive father. It was his direct connection with Washington that made individuals seek out his company. For thirty years Custis wrote newspaper accounts of the daily life of Washington and his family. Upon his own death in 1857, the country mourned the loss of the man who'd maintained their connection to Washington.

This daguerreotype by renowned photographer Mathew Brady shows Custis in a white waistcoat, confident and relaxed in front of the camera. A tentative date for the image suggests that it was taken between 1844 and 1849, perhaps while Custis was on his national tour.

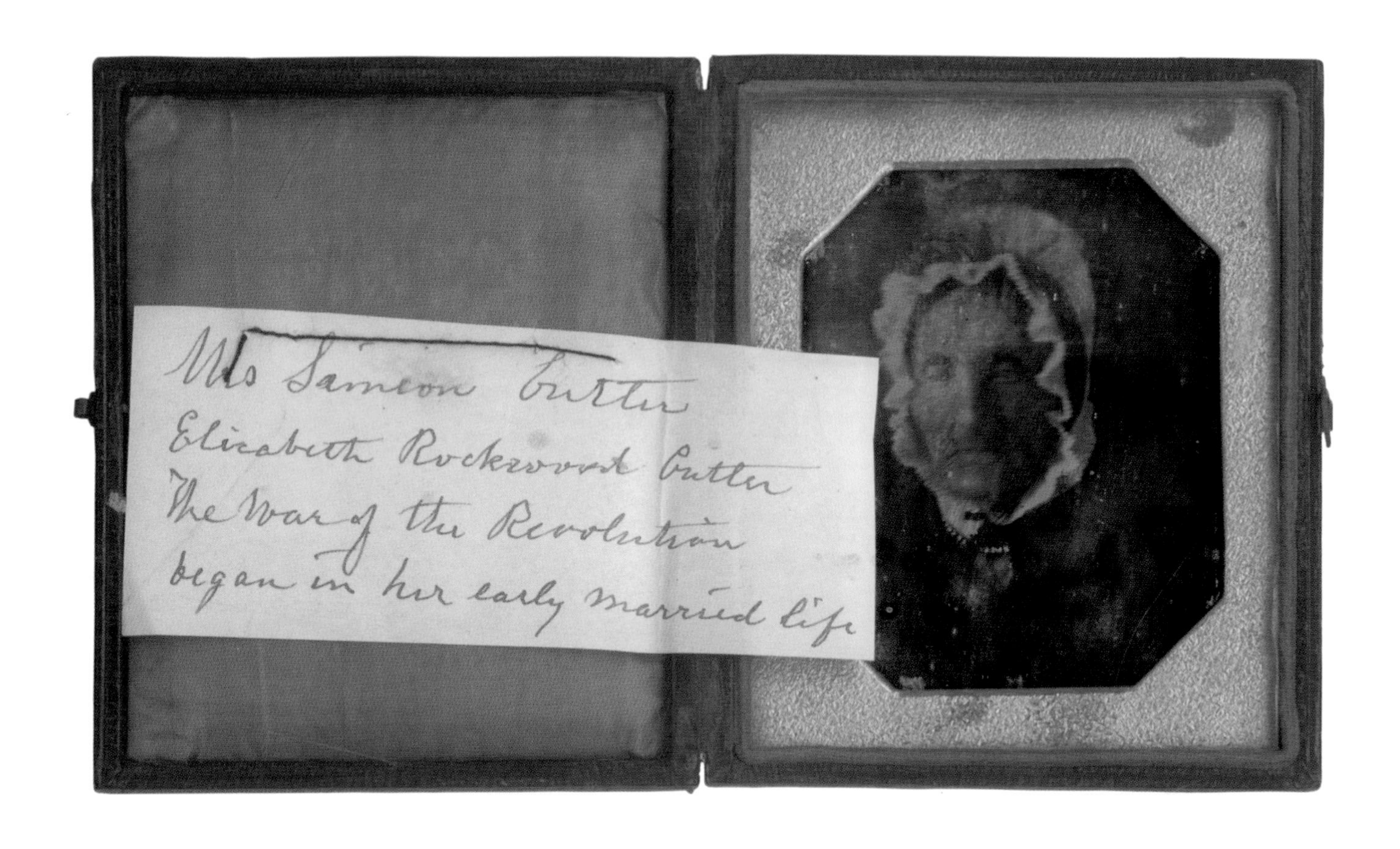
Mrs Samson Cutter
Elizabeth Rockwood Cutter
The War of the Revolution
began in her early married life

Elizabeth Cutler (December 23, 1753–May 1849)
New England Historic Genealogical Society

A simple handwritten note is sewn to the fabric liner in this cased image. It reads "Mrs. Simeon Cutler, Elisabeth Rockwood Cutler. The War of the Revolution began in her early married life." In this daguerreotype taken in the 1840s while she was in her nineties, Cutler looks down and away from the camera lens, giving her the appearance of being sad or contemplative.

Elizabeth Rockwood, born December 23, 1753, married Simeon Cutler, the "boy next door," in Holliston, Massachusetts, in approximately 1770 when she was seventeen years of age. The couple ran a public house at the Cutler Homestead, which her husband inherited at the age of thirteen.

Their early married years were consumed by Revolutionary politics. Her husband held a pivotal role devising strategies for defending towns in their area and was a minuteman, ready to serve at a moment's notice. During the conflict, with Simeon away in the service, Elizabeth found herself charged with managing the farm, running the tavern, and caring for two young children. It is no wonder a genealogy of the family described her as a "woman of rare energy and moral worth." She kept the Cutler Inn solvent despite the financial vagaries of war, which closed most of their competitors.

After the war, Simeon became colonel of the militia for Holliston. The couple continued to operate their farm and inn, adding a variety store and later a wheelwright shop for their son, Elihu. Her husband died in 1798, leaving her a widow for half a century until her death in 1849.

According to the terms of Simeon's will, as was the custom of the era, Elizabeth received one-third of his estate, with the remainder going to their children. She received the right to use the front room, the cellar beneath it, half of the room adjacent to the front room, and half of the garret above that. The will specifically outlined that she would receive one-half of her husband's "right in the Meetinghouse and liberty to do her work in the kitching [*sic*] and backroom of the dwelling," rights to part of the yard and use of the well, as well as the new end of the barn. After her death, her descendants remarked, "By industry and good management of her property, she was not only able to provide a comfortable and independent support, but also to contribute to many benevolent objects." This subdued portrait of an elderly woman in a day cap from her youth doesn't begin to capture her strength of character.

Esther Damon (April 1, 1814–November 11, 1906)
Daughters of the American Revolution

An ordinary woman from Vermont holds the distinction of being the "Last Widow of the Revolution." When seventy-five-year-old Noah Damon proposed to Esther Sumner in 1835, the townspeople of Bridgewater, Vermont, were likely surprised. Sumner was only twenty-one. It was his second marriage and her first. Though it may seem a strange union today, it was not unusual for a woman to marry a veteran who had the prospect of pension support.

Damon, like Esther's grandfather, had served in the American Revolution. As a boy under sixteen years of age, Damon served for five days with the Milton Minute Company at the Battle of Lexington and Concord. A year later he was drafted for three months' service with Gen. George Washington's army in the New York City area where he received a bayonet wound to his right thigh. Over the course of the war he served several more times in a variety of capacities and participated in the Battle of Newport, Rhode Island, in 1778.

Esther Sumner became his second wife on September 6, 1835. Their life together was difficult due to Noah's advanced age and feeble condition. The town of Bridgewater provided financial assistance for Noah but not for Esther, who the town government declared "able to care of herself" (Wickman, "Last Widow," C-4). In the late 1840s the couple separated. Noah went to live with one of his daughters while Esther stayed in Bridgewater. It appears to have been an acrimonious separation, for when he finally applied for a pension at the age of eighty-nine in 1848, using his scar as evidence of his service, Damon never mentioned in his application that he had a wife. When he died on July 2, 1854, Esther Damon became a widow eligible for a pension.

Esther hired an attorney to help with her 1855 pension claim. Her mother, Elizabeth Frink, testified regarding her daughter's marriage to Damon. In the deposition, Frink stated that Damon wouldn't support her daughter so that she had to find employment to support herself. Her mother also related how, after Esther Damon saved some of her earnings, the town of Bridgewater, Vermont, claimed them to cover maintenance expenses generated by her husband. Her petition for a pension was successful, and she received eighty dollars per year as long as she remained single.

Esther Damon never remarried, instead moving to live with her elderly mother in Plymouth, Vermont. She later became a member of the Daughters of the American Revolution through her grandfather's service. In 1904, her fellow members sought further financial support for her from the Vermont legislature. In the special act passed in Vermont, Damon was referred to as "the last surviving widow of a revolutionary soldier." The Committee of Pensions under Congress granted a pension increase to twenty-four dollars per month because of her "distinction of being the sole surviving widow pensioner of the Revolutionary War."

This photograph appeared in Merrit L. Dawkins, "The Sands of Time," *Daughters of the American Revolution Report* (1907–8).

Simon Dearborn (November 20, 1760–July 17, 1853)
Collections of Maine Historical Society

Simon Dearborn, a struggling farmer in Maine, married twice and had seven children, the youngest when he was fifty-two. A son of Simon and Anna (Sanborn) Dearborn, he was born in New Hampshire.

While in his initial pension claim in 1818 he said he first enlisted in 1777, he actually appears on a muster roll for Capt. James Norris's Company, Col. Enoch Poor's 2nd New Hampshire Regiment, in 1775. At fifteen he was the youngest member of that company. He remained in the service until 1779, discharged at a place he could no longer recall as of 1818. He reported that he served with General (John) Sullivan, who led campaigns against the Tutelo tribe that sided with the British, and perhaps this is what Dearborn referred to in his descriptions of fighting the Indians in his pension claim. Dearborn was with Sullivan when Gen. John Burgoyne surrendered to the Americans at Saratoga, New York, in October 1777. Dearborn received a pension for his years of service with Capt. Michael McClary's Company in Col. Alexander Scammel's 3rd New Hampshire Regiment.

As a recipient of a pension in 1818, he had to reapply in 1820. At that time his total worth was $230, comprising various farm animals and household belongings outside of "necessary bedding." The court valued his fifty acres and improvements at $500. He claimed to be infirm and able to do little work. At home he lived with his rheumatic wife, Mehitable, and two sons, Ebenezer (22) and Henry (7), as well as a daughter, Dorcas (24).

In 1824, Dearborn stated that he conveyed his land to his son Greenleaf, "who had advanced sums of money for my support & that of my family & also he had paid debts against me some of which were of long standing." Dearborn explained, "My situation at this time is as I have represented in my second schedule, being destitute of property and now in my sixty fourth year of my age. I served three full years in the War of the Revolution and from my reduced circumstances in life stand in need of the assistance of my country for support" (Pension Records).

Dearborn died when he was ninety-two years seven months old. In this daguerreotype, probably taken in the 1850s, his light eyes, white hair, and neck scarf tied neatly around his collar lend dignity to this portrait.

Samuel Downing (c. 1764–February 18, 1867)
Reverend E. B. Hillard, The Last Men of the Revolution

When Rev. Elias Hillard set out to interview the last seven surviving Revolutionary War soldiers for his book *The Last Men of the Revolution,* the first man he visited was Samuel Downing.

Downing's tale had a sad beginning. As a young boy, his parents, David Downing and Susanna Beacham Downing, left him home alone when a man named Thomas Aiken approached him, offering education and other enticements if the boy came with him. Downing left home to live with Aiken's family, laboring on his farm but never receiving the education he'd been promised. The American Revolution was an opportunity for Downing to run away from his captor. He remembered being too young to enlist in 1776, but officials let him once they'd heard his story. He remained in the army until discharged in 1783. Downing's pension file provides details of his service with the 2nd Regiment New Hampshire line as a private under the command of Capt. John Dennett and Col. George Reid. He received a pension under the Act of 1818 and two parcels of bounty land—one hundred acres on March 22, 1796, and sixty acres in 1855.

During the course of his visit with Hillard, Downing recollected escapades with fellow privates such as stealing rum from the officers. He also described the generals he met. Serving with Benedict Arnold in New York, he remembered him as brave, dark skinned, thin, and kind to his soldiers. George Washington was nice but never smiled.

An obituary in the *Pittsfield (Massachusetts) Sun* recounted Downing's wartime experiences, including allegedly witnessing "the capitulation of Burgoyne on the 17th of October [1777], and . . . the surrender of 5[,]752 British soldiers and 5,000 British muskets to Gen. Schuyler." Like a lot of the pensioners, Downing recalled being present at many of the key moments of the war.

After the war he returned to the Aikens, married, and soon left with a group of individuals seeking opportunities in upstate New York. Downing built the first frame house in Edinburgh, New York, for his wife and thirteen children. On his one hundredth birthday, he was given a new axe and proceeded to cut down a hemlock tree twenty-two inches in diameter and a black cherry tree, proving that he was still fit despite being a centenarian. His year of birth is uncertain: he claimed it was 1761, but in other reports it was listed as several years later. He was, however, definitely over one hundred years of age when he died in 1867. This photograph was taken during Hillard's visit, years before Downing's death.

Pierre Etienne DuPonceau (June 3, 1760–April 1, 1844) also known as Peter Stephen DuPonceau
American Philosophical Society

In 1777 the seventeen-year-old French-born DuPonceau accompanied Baron von Steuben to America, serving as his secretary, aide-de-camp, and translator. Benjamin Franklin introduced the Prussian-trained von Steuben to Gen. George Washington as a "Lieutenant General in the King of Prussia's Army," but that was a fallacy. Despite von Steuben's dubious credentials, he was hired to develop a training program for American troops with assistance from Alexander Hamilton and Gen. Nathanael Greene. He picked a hundred men for a unit and, although he spoke only French and German, managed to teach them military techniques. DuPonceau translated von Steuben's German into English. These men in turn trained the rest of the army. Von Steuben's techniques evidently worked, as demonstrated by American successes on the battlefields. Washington appointed him major general inspector general, and his aide, DuPonceau, became a captain in the Continental Army, swearing an oath of allegiance. Both were with Washington at Valley Forge. DuPonceau continued with his secretarial duties to von Steuben and published, in 1779, *Regulations for the Order and Discipline of the Troops of the United States.* He translated von Steuben's manual of arms into French and English. DuPonceau ended the war as a major.

In 1794, he applied for and was awarded a land grant of three hundred acres on January 21, 1794, for his service. In 1828 he applied for additional assistance, claiming he'd received five years of full pension as of the resolve of March 22, 1783, but nothing as of March 3, 1826. There was a dispute over DuPonceau's eligibility for a pension under the 1828 act due to the fact that he was a foreign officer. Letters support his claim that, as an American citizen, he was entitled to the pension. His pension file contains a letter from 1843 in which DuPonceau requested a raise from $480 a year to $600, an amount that far exceeded the pension payments received by ordinary soldiers. It was a successful bid for additional support.

DuPonceau remained in the United States after the war, serving as secretary to the U.S. secretary of foreign affairs, Robert Livingston, his duties focusing on international law and trade. He married Anne la Touche on September 12, 1794, at Trinity Church Parish in New York City.

As a linguist, DuPonceau knew several European languages and also studied Native American languages. His information on Indian linguistics is still referenced today. He joined the American Philosophical Society in 1791 and became president of the organization in 1827, a position he held until his death on April 1, 1844. In 1831 he spoke to the Law Academy of Philadelphia about the Constitution of the United States: "Thus we have presented to our readers a brief view of the constitution of the United States, which, on cool and mature reflection, we cannot help considering as the most perfect system of government that has ever existed among mankind" (DuPonceau, *Brief View of the Constitution,* 47).

In the early 1840s DuPonceau posed for this daguerreotype by Robert Cornelius of Philadelphia. Its ethereal quality highlights his forehead and cheeks, but hides his eyes behind dark glasses.

Ralph Farnham (July 7, 1756–December 16, 1860)
Massachusetts Historical Society

For his 102nd birthday, Ralph Farnham sat for this ambrotype portrait. He looks down at the floor rather than at the photographer, tightly holding his cane, perhaps a little nervous about this new process. Ambrotypes were first patented by Robert Cutting in 1854, just four years earlier. These images on glass were presented to customers in cases.

This humble farmer joined the patriotic movement in 1775 with a group of local boys serving with Col. James Scamman who called themselves the "Yorkshire lads," as they resided in York County, Maine. These fresh recruits, dressed in their own clothing and armed with their own rifles, rushed to Boston in hopes of participating in the rebellion. They camped at Cambridge with other troops and were sent, not to Bunker Hill in Charlestown, but to East Cambridge, because rumor suggested that the British were going to land there. Eventually ordered to help at "the hill," referring to what would be known as the Battle of Bunker Hill, Scamman misunderstood and took them to the wrong place. By the time they arrived at the real battle, the fighting was over and the Americans were in retreat. As their commanding officer, Scamman was tried for court-martial for disobeying orders but was acquitted. Farnham and his compatriots served until December 1775.

Once home Farnham reenlisted, but this time as a member of the York County militia, which enabled him to train for battle while maintaining the family farm. During the remainder of the Revolution he served two more stints—drafted for two and a half months as a second sergeant in Capt. Samuel Grant's Company under Col. Benjamin Titcomb in Rhode Island and for four months with Capt. Elisha Shapleigh of Maine. During his assignment with Captain Shapleigh, he was present in Saratoga for British general John Burgoyne's surrender. He mustered out in December 1777 and spent the rest of the war in Acton, Maine. Farnham received a pension for his service in 1833 and 160 acres of bounty land in New Hampshire in 1855 when he was ninety-nine years old.

Even though not technically present at the Battle of Bunker Hill, he became associated with the event and was proclaimed by newspapers as the last survivor of that battle. C. W. Lawrence published *A Biographical Sketch of the Life of Ralph Farnham of Acton, Maine* in September 1860 with the following note: "Mr. Farnham's Yearly Pension, upon which he is dependent for support, is only $61.66 and these Books are sold for his benefit." Also offered at the same time was a single sheet featuring a headshot of Farnham, his autograph, and another announcement about all profits going to help support him financially.

On Independence Day 1860, orator Edward Everett Hale gave a speech in Boston proclaiming that there were no survivors of the American Revolution. The citizens of Acton, Maine, sent him a letter correcting his mistake by telling him about Farnham. To honor his 104th birthday that year, his hometown held an event and brought this Revolutionary

War veteran national fame. Local folk called him "Uncle Farnham" and celebrated his wartime service and his centenarian status with a 104-gun salute, speeches, and a dinner. It was a spectacle worthy of a world leader. Newspapers across the country picked up the story.

In October 1860, Boston dignitaries sent him a letter: "We desire to see you—to shake hands with you, and to pay you that respect due alike to your patriarchal age, and to the part you took in the struggle which secured our National Independence." In his reply, he remarked, "I receive every year my pension of $61.66, though I have to pay a lawyer $4 for me to get it." He stayed for at least ten days at city expense to attend a concert in his honor and was given a tour of the city by the Prince of Wales. At the time he remarked humorously that "he had heard so much in praise of the Prince that he feared the people of his country were all turning Royalists" (*New England Tour of His Royal Highness*). Visitors could sign a subscription book and present him with a monetary gift. He collected about seventy-five dollars.

At the time of visit, the *New York Herald* reported that "the old warrior is still vigorous, and does not seem near so old as he really is." He died on December 26, 1860.

Sarah (Stevens) Fellows (November 26, 1762–July 1863)
Courtesy of Gayle Waite

Several months after the death of her husband in 1846, eighty-four-year-old Sarah Stevens Fellows applied for the widow's benefits owed her. She produced a marriage record signed by the town clerk in Salisbury, New Hampshire, to show that she had married Revolutionary War pensioner Moses Fellows on May 20, 1782. She recounted for the court a summary of her husband's service, made her mark at the bottom of the document, and successfully obtained her pension.

Moses Fellows enlisted in 1775 as a private in Captain Hale's Company, Colonel Stark's New Hampshire Regiment, and had been in the Battle of Bunker Hill. It's unclear which Stark and which regiment. The *History of Salisbury, New Hampshire* contains a story about his time on that battlefield: "Moses, in his twentieth year, fought at Bunker Hill, at which time a ball fired by the British cut off the cord to which his powder horn was suspended. With his last charge of powder and no ball, he fired his ramrod with such precision as to kill one of the enemy." In his original pension application in 1819, he outlined how he had served with Capt. Henry Dearborn's Company in Quebec in 1775 and was in the Battle of Quebec under the direction of Col. Benedict Arnold.

He enlisted again in April 1777 as a corporal and sergeant in Capt. James Gray's Company in Col. Alexander Scammel's New Hampshire Regiment, serving until 1780. His 1819 pension application was successful. He received a pension retroactive to May 1818 but was dropped from the rolls in 1820. While he had previously received a pension for a private, he appealed in 1832, "My wish now is to be placed on the pension list as a Sergeant under the last act of Congress, June 7, 1832" (Pension Records). He was successful.

After the war he married Sarah, daughter of Reuben Stevens, and raised seven children. She survived her husband by nineteen years. According to Dearborn's history of the town, "On her one hundredth birthday, she gave a party to her large circle of friends, who were the oldest people in town. She attributed her long life to a good constitution, regular habits and early rising."

In this card photograph taken perhaps to commemorate her centenarian status, she's hunched over with age, peering away from the camera with her day cap neatly tied under her chin. She died a year later.

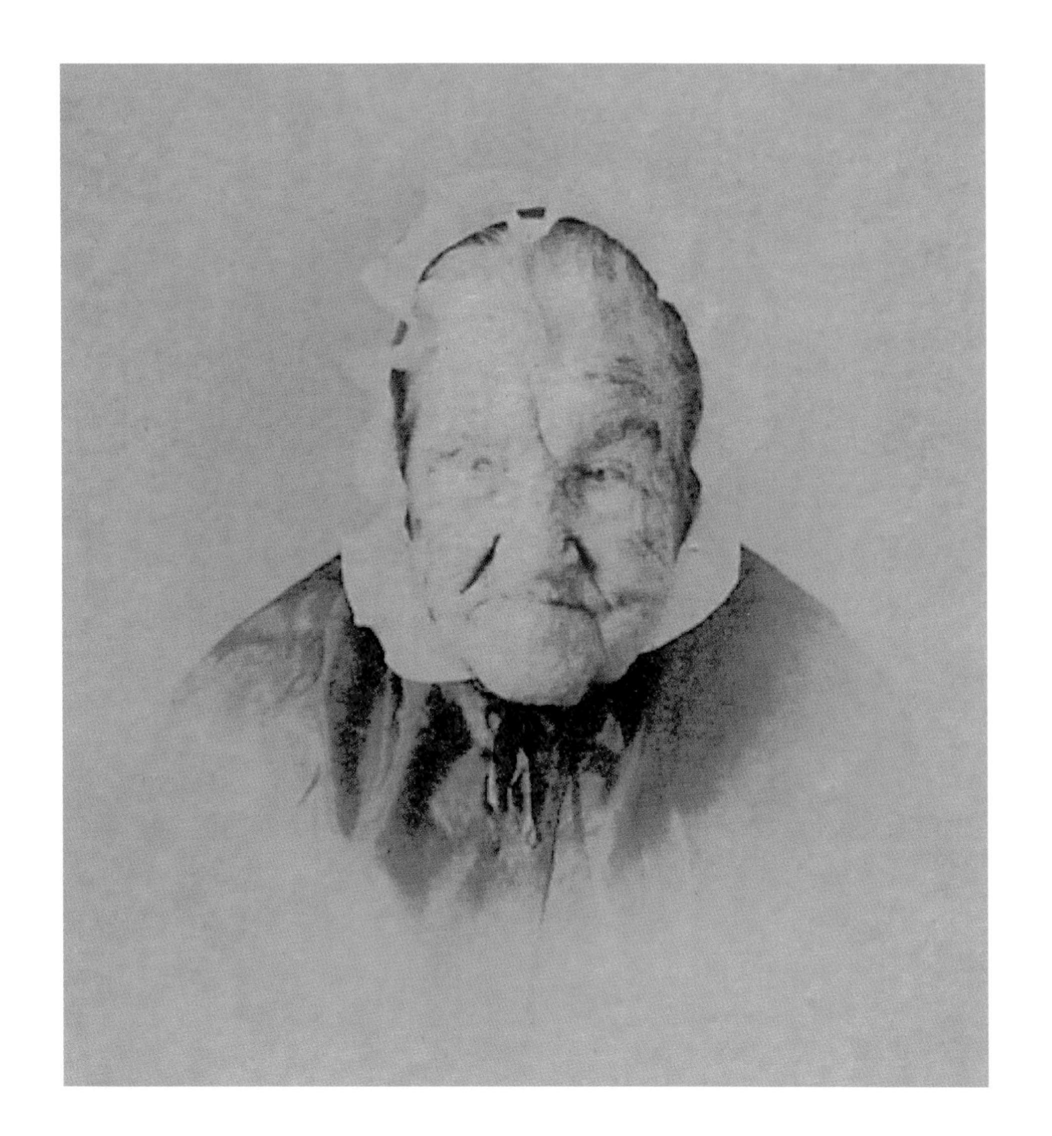

George Fishley (June 17, 1760–December 26, 1851)
Collection of the Portsmouth (NH) Historical Society

The blurring in this daguerreotype is the result of Fishley's moving during the capturing of the image. It's essentially a photographer's proof. There are at least four known images of him. All were probably taken on the same day. This version was recently rediscovered in the collections of the Portsmouth (New Hampshire) Historical Society. All depict Fishley in a uniform with his oversize hat atop his head. He proudly poses for this portrait. His blue eyes are barely visible. The handwritten label reads, "Capt.n George Fishley is 90 years on this his birthday June 11, 1850. He called at the house this afternoon[.] he appeared well & hearty for an old man. December 24th 1850 this Evening went to sleep and died. December 26th 1850 Aged 90 years 7 months and 15 days. Written by George Pearse of Portsmouth, N.H. son of Stephen & Sarah H. Peabody Pearse. G. Pearse died 1868. Susan Woodman."

In 1847, Fishley was among the three surviving Revolutionary War veterans that met President Polk during his visit to Portsmouth in July of that year. The other two veterans were Mark Green and George Long, both also in their eighties. At the time, Portsmouth had six Revolutionary War veterans living in the area. Fishley's image is the only identified daguerreotype of these six men. His attire in this daguerreotype was explained in the *Portsmouth Journal* after his death: "For many years he has on public occasions appeared conspicuously in the processions in a cocked-hat which almost vied in years with the wearer."

A summary of Fishley's Revolutionary War service on land and sea appeared in his testimony for his pension application and was recounted in a memorial piece in the *Portsmouth Journal* on January 4, 1851. Born in 1760, he became a private in the Continental Army at seventeen in 1776, serving with General Poor and Colonel Dearborn for New Hampshire. He spent three years in service for New Hampshire and claimed that he was at the Battle of Monmouth, "in actions in the Indian Country under Genl. Sullivan, and was present at the execution of Major Andre" (Pension Records). In the last years of his life Fishley also reported that he marched without shoes and stockings with his comrades during the winter at Valley Forge. At the conclusion of his service, he became a privateer and was taken prisoner and held at Halifax, Nova Scotia. He spent the rest of his working life on the water, trading goods and operating his own coaster, a shallow-hulled ship, between Portsmouth, New Hampshire, and Boston.

On May 5, 1839, the *Portsmouth Journal of Literature and Politics* printed a notice that Capt. George Fishley's wife had died and that he "in the space of one short week has been bereft of a wife and an only daughter."

The account of his life in the *Portsmouth Journal* contained two anecdotes that provide insight into his character. During Polk's visit to Portsmouth, Fishley, a Whig supporter, "said he declined at first shaking hands with him, because he had no political sympathies with him." A few years earlier, the Whig Party had met in Concord, and Fishley had appeared at the meeting along with three hundred other Portsmouth residents. "As an emblem of commerce, a miniature

ship was rigged, and was drawn from our wharves to the political capital of the State. The commander of this vessel, which will be long remembered, was Capt. Fishley." In closing, the *Portsmouth Journal* said, "Incorporated in his very existence was the spirit of '76—and on all fitting occasions it was prominently visible. With him the last of our cocked hats has departed."

Albert Gallatin (January 29, 1761–August 13, 1849)
Library of Congress

Orphaned as a child and dependent on extended family for financial support, Gallatin ran away from his birthplace of Geneva, Switzerland, to seek his fortune in America, arriving in Boston on July 14, 1780. This university-educated immigrant viewed the American Revolution as a mistake and yet thought he'd profit enough in this country to become an independent man. According to his obituary in the *Farmer's Cabinet,* shortly after Gallatin's arrival "he served as a volunteer under Col. John Allan, commander of the fort of Machias [Maine]; and also made some advances to support the garrison." In his early years in the United States, during the latter years of the war, Gallatin tried to sell tea in Boston, traded with Indians in Maine, and marginally supported himself teaching Harvard students French.

After the war Gallatin thought that the western frontier offered better financial opportunities so, together with Jean Savary de Valcoulon, who was a French land agent, he bought acreage along the Ohio River in Pennsylvania and Virginia. They looked on these purchases as investments, with the expectation that immigrants and eastern farmers would want to move to the area. While this didn't bring Gallatin business success, it did offer him a chance to enter politics.

By the time of his election as a delegate to a political convention at Harrisburg, Pennsylvania, Gallatin backed the founding principles of his adopted country. He served three terms in the Pennsylvania House of Representatives. He was a supporter of small business and a critic of Alexander Hamilton, who at the time was U.S. treasurer. When elected to the U.S. Senate in 1793, the Senate denied him access, supposedly because he hadn't been a citizen for nine years. In 1795 he ran again and served for six years in the House of Representatives on a platform that criticized the Federalists, a move that placed him in the political arena with James Madison and Thomas Jefferson. Some biographers credit him with getting Thomas Jefferson elected president. Gallatin's publications and positions on U.S. financial policy made him a logical choice to become secretary of the treasury in 1801, beginning with Jefferson's first term of office and continuing until 1812.

His list of accomplishments included negotiating the Treaty of Ghent, serving as U.S minister to France (1816–23), settling the boundary between the United States and Canada (1818), and serving as president of the National Bank of New York (1831–39). He continued to publish pamphlets on U.S. finances and political and ethnographic topics, such as the Mexican War and Indian tribes in this country. Recognized as an intellectual, he helped establish New York University and became the first president of the American Ethnological Society and the New-York Historical Society.

As of 1848, Gallatin was ill and bedridden. He died in August 1849. In this daguerreotype, probably taken by Anthony, Edwards and Co. and copied by Mathew B. Brady, Gallatin poses with humor and intelligence visible in his eyes.

John Gray (January 6, 1764–March 29, 1868)
Library of Congress

According to his biographer, James McCormick Dalzell, the poor and proud John Gray wouldn't apply for support until he was one hundred years of age. Born January 6, 1764, near George Washington's estate of Mount Vernon, he lived to be 102, dying on March 29, 1868.

On December 3, 1866, the Honorable John A. Bingham, a member of the House of Representatives, introduced a special bill for financial aid for Gray. It asked the secretary of the interior to provide a pension of two hundred dollars a year payable semiannually. Mr. Price of the Committee on Revolutionary War Pensions testified, "This applicant is one hundred and three years old, and I have another similar case to report, in which the applicant is one hundred and seven years old (referring to Daniel Frederick Bakeman) and both these men are supported by public charity" (Dalzell, *John Gray, of Mount Vernon,* 5). Beginning on July 1, 1866, Gray received five hundred dollars a year for life. Dalzell's account not only provides a biography of Gray but offers support for his claim of being the next to the last living Revolutionary War veteran. Dalzell offers that Gray was a common man without documentation for his life, so the only resource for his book is Gray's personal recollections. However, Gray's pension application details his military service. In it, he claimed to first enlist in the militia as a private in February 1781 (until May 1781) in Capt. Robert Sanford's Company in Colonel Church's Regiment.

Dalzell says that he undertook this biographical project so that he could talk with the one man who could say, "I have shaken hands with Washington and fought under him. I was born at Mount Vernon and was his warm personal friend" (Dalzell, *John Gray, of Mount Vernon,* 8). Dalzell found Gray sitting at home chewing tobacco and remarking on his Christian values. Gray could read and write and remembered writing to his mother from the battlefield. Gray reminisced that he was one of Washington's favorite soldiers.

During the Revolution, Gray claimed to have remained at home helping his mother care for the younger children while his father served. He joined the army at eighteen in time to be at the Battle of Yorktown. Other accounts suggest that after his father died at the Battle of White Plains, New York, Gray enlisted, carrying his father's musket. The latter is probably true. He told Dalzell, "I was a mighty tough kind of a boy in them days, I tell you. I saw big, heavy men give out, but I never lagged a foot behind. . . . When we were near Williamsburg[,] orders came to send out a scouting party to feel of the British, who were then trying to come up to Williamsburg. We were too weak to fight them. But our captain called for volunteers to go out on a scrimmage, and I volunteered with sixty others. We had gone only two or three miles when we came upon the red-coats, in large force." The men fell back, outmanned and outgunned at that point. About a year later Cornwallis surrendered at Yorktown. According to his declaration in his pension application, Gray told the examiner that he served from February to May 1781 in Capt. Robert Sanford's Company in Colonel Church's Regiment and that he served again from June to October 19, 1781, in Capt. James Neal's Company.

One of the anecdotes that Gray told Dalzell took place at Mount Vernon after the war. One day as Gary worked alongside Washington's slaves, thinking about his Revolutionary War service, Washington came by on horseback and called to him. They reportedly shook hands, and Washington asked about his health and told him not to work too hard.

Gray married three times—twice in Virginia and once after his move to Ohio in 1795. He outlived all three of his wives, and only one daughter, with whom he lived at the time of his death, outlived him.

At the end of the book, Dalzell confessed that he knew Gray as a neighbor for twenty years: "I loved him because he had fought for the same flag that I had, and I loved him because he was so much like Washington—plain, simple, honest, and good. . . . His name should not and cannot rot in oblivion."

After Gray's death, newspapers mourned the loss of the last Revolutionary War soldier. Photographer I. N. Knowlton wrote to Dalzell that he had Gray's photograph and autograph copyrighted but lacked the exact date he received his pension and would like to place it on the back of the image. The carte de visite photo depicted here is the one mentioned in that letter.

Dr. Ezra Green (June 17, 1746–July 25, 1847)
Collection of David Allen Lambert

In 1845, the ninety-nine-year-old Green held the distinction of being the oldest living Harvard University graduate. Born in 1746 he graduated with the class of 1765. At that time, the study of medicine was a profession often learned from a more experienced physician, and Green began studying with Dr. John Spraque of Newburyport, Massachusetts. By 1767, Green had his own practice in Dover, New Hampshire, and became a leading member of the community until the Battle of Bunker Hill in 1775. In 1776, Green became the surgeon of James Reed's 2nd Continental Regiment in Gen. John Sullivan's brigade.

According to his pension application of 1832, he traveled from Albany to Ticonderoga, and his company joined Benedict Arnold in Montreal during that officer's fall back from Quebec. Green continued to care for troops in his unit until he was discharged in December 1776. At six foot three inches tall, Green was often mistaken by fellow soldiers for Gen. George Washington, both for his stature and for his demeanor.

After his discharge, Green remained at home for close to a year, until he received a commission in October 1777 to serve as ship's surgeon on John Paul Jones's eighteen-gun "ship-of-war," the *Ranger.* It was newly built on Langdon's Island in Portsmouth harbor, New Hampshire, and Green joined it on its first voyage. There were 140 men on board in April 1778. Their first stop was France, followed by trips along the coast of England. Every day, from November 1, 1777, to September 27, 1778, Green kept a diary of his life on board the *Ranger.* At times he commented on the weather or detailed ships they chased. Noted are deaths of shipmates, names of deserters, and entertainments such as visits by ladies or shore-leave trips to the theater.

On the return voyage, Jones remained in France and left command of the ship to his first officer, Lt. Thomas Simpson. At home around Christmas of 1778, Green found time to marry Susanna Hayes on December 30. Newspaper accounts of the time recount, "In the spring of 1779 he went on a cruise with Captain Simpson in the *Ranger,* in company with the warships, The *Providence* and the *Queen of France.* They encountered six brigs loaded with salt, under convoy of a brig of fourteen guns, and took them all in Portsmouth, New Hampshire" (*Farmer's Cabinet,* Sept. 11, 1845). On another voyage they took seven of a Jamaica fleet full of rum, sugar, logwood, pimento, and other goods to Boston. In this case, "as they approached the harbor, the house-tops were crowded with people, alarmed at the sight of ten large ships coming up, supposing them to be a British fleet" (*Farmer's Cabinet,* Sept. 11, 1845).

In October 1779, after two years with the *Ranger,* Green left the service, briefly returning home to Dover, New Hampshire. In the next year he served at sea on the *Alexan-*

der. Family tradition suggests that he retired from medicine, but as of 1807 he was still involved with the New Hampshire Medical Society.

Green held a number of different positions after the war—doctor, tavern keeper, retailer, local politician, church warden, justice of the peace, and postmaster. He was made the first postmaster of Dover in 1790. He didn't begin to receive a pension until 1833. A stroke in 1836 left him unable to walk, and in his pension file is a letter from his daughter Susan in support of an increase of his annual payment: "The old Gentleman is bordering on the age of 100. His spine being affected he requires constant attendance." Green died in 1847, aged 101.

Although the location of the original daguerreotype of Dr. Ezra Green is currently unknown, two copies of it exist, an engraving in an 1875 publication of his diary and the enhanced carte de visite by E. T. Brigham's Studio in Dover, New Hampshire, reproduced here. The photographer enhanced Green's eyes and hair with charcoal pencil. Green sits in a rocking chair.

Josiah Walpole Hall (December 16, 1753–July 15, 1855)
Courtesy of Phillip Burcham

Someone, probably a relative, decided in the late nineteenth century to copy the original daguerreotype of Josiah Hall. He took it to George S. Raymond's studio in Ogdensburg, New York, and his descendants are glad he did. This paper photograph is all that's left; the location of the cased image is unknown. On the back of this picture is a caption: "Josiah Hall, born in Walpole, Mass., Dec. 16, 1753, died in Walpole, Mass., July 15, 1855." It's a sparse description for a man who had a key role in the events of April 19, 1775.

According to material in family hands, the twenty-two-year-old Hall reportedly traveled the road from Walpole to Concord, Massachusetts, to warn that General Gage's regulars were crossing the Charles River to march to Lexington and Concord. They were on their way to arrest Samuel Adams and John Hancock and to capture military supplies at Concord. Gage's informants gave him the exact location.

As a recipient of a pension under the Act of 1818, he reapplied in 1820, providing proof of his need and enumerating the value of his assets and debts as well as a list of those dependent on him. He included the name of his sister, Rebecca (aged sixty-four) as "weakly lame," his daughter Miranda (aged nineteen) as "sickly and unable to support herself," and a daughter Calla who "was able to support herself" (Pension Records). About himself he said, "I'm a farmer by occupation considerably debilitated by age and unable to perform one half the labor of a common man." He was dropped from the rolls in 1820.

In 1832 he restates his service. Hall mentions enlisting as a private in May 1775 in Capt. Seth Bullard's company of Massachusetts Continentals and camping at Roxbury near Boston for a service that lasted eight months. He testified that in the early months of 1776 he reenlisted, spending more time in Roxbury and Dorchester, then marched through Providence, Rhode Island, and New London, Connecticut, to finally arrive in New York City as part of Capt. Joseph Read's Regiment. Several individuals give depositions in support of his application, saying that they had served with him. The first mention of his actions on April 19, 1775, appears in an 1846 pension document. It states that his name appears on a "muster roll of Capt. Seth Bullard's Company of militia in Walpole, in Col. John Smith's regt., on an alarm" (Pension Records). On that day, Hall was reinstated and received an increase in his pension for the additional ten days' service.

Even though the January 6, 1855, *Boston Evening Transcript* announced his good health on his 101st birthday, it was only a matter of months until he died.

This picture of Hall sat in family files until a few years ago, when descendants rediscovered it. One of his descendants recently wrote, "It seems incredible that we have an image of our ancestor who took part in the American Revolution" (e-mail from Phillip Burcham).

J. SIMPSON.

Jonathan Harrington (July 8, 1758–March 26, 1854)
From the Collection of the Lexington, Massachusetts, Historical Society

Imagine the excitement of Jonathan Harrington on the morning of April 19, 1775. At seventeen he was the youngest member of Capt. John Parker's company of minutemen. It was his job to play the fife when the soldiers crossed the North Bridge at the Battle of Lexington and Concord. Harrington was there with his father, brother, and three cousins. It would be Harrington's only military service in the war.

Benson Lossing toured the country in 1848 while compiling his *Field-Book of the American Revolution,* and he was able to visit with the ninety-year-old Harrington at his home in Lexington, Massachusetts. When Lossing arrived, Harrington was splitting firewood in his yard. As Lossing sketched him, he marveled that Harrington looked no more than seventy. As they finished talking, Harrington's brother, Caleb, arrived. Lossing was awed to be in the company of two men who were present at the first battle of the Revolution.

In 1850 Harrington was among the veterans honored at the seventy-fifth anniversary celebration of the events of April 1775. He eventually outlived them all, becoming the last survivor of the "shot heard round the world." When he died in 1854, at ninety-five years of age, newspapers reported that thousands of people witnessed his funeral procession as it passed by the monuments draped in mourning. A full order of procession appeared in the *Boston Evening Transcript.* It included military companies and fraternal organizations. The entire procession and services didn't end until five o'clock in the evening. This was a testament to the patriotic fervor and honor surrounding this man.

This daguerreotype by John Stimpson was taken in the early 1850s, when Stimpson had studios in Boston, Cambridge, and Cambridgeport, Massachusetts. It depicts the long-haired Harrington as a very elderly man of some infirmities. He doesn't look completely comfortable in front of the camera.

Conrad Heyer (April 10, 1753–February 19, 1856)
Collections of the Maine Historical Society

Conrad Heyer was the first white child born in Waldoboro, Maine, then a German immigrant community. He was raised by his mother, as his father had died during the winter before his birth. A recent genealogical study of the German settlers of Waldoboro suggests that he was born in 1753. He was also known as Cornelius. In 1772–73, his mother, Catharina, married another German immigrant, David Holzappel, and moved with him to a Moravian community in North Carolina. In 1776, Heyer married Mary Webber. They had ten children.

The *History of Waldoboro, Maine* contains a biographical sketch of Heyer, stating that throughout his youth he had been an active member of the German Lutheran Church there and was one of the singers at its dedication. He left town during the American Revolution to serve as a private in Colonel Bond's Massachusetts Line, helping to build Fort Ticonderoga as a member of the Continental Army. He crossed the Delaware with Washington and survived the winter at Valley Forge, Pennsylvania. At one time he served as a member of Washington's guard. Heyer was one of the men present at the surrender of General Burgoyne at Saratoga.

He applied for a pension under the legislation of 1818, and as of 1820 this farmer owned no real estate, only one ox, two cows, and some old furniture. Both he and his wife were infirm and being cared for by their daughter. He made his mark on his application, being unable to sign his name. Heyer applied for bounty land at the age of 106 in 1855.

After the war he returned to Waldoboro, where he died at the age of 106 years 10 months 9 days, living longer than any other resident of the town up to that time.

It's unknown when Heyer posed for this daguerreotype. With suspicious and steady eyes, he tilts his head toward the photographer. His somewhat puckered mouth suggests that he's missing some upper teeth. Whatever he thought of having his picture taken, he dressed neatly: in the likeness his vest buttons catch the light, and the natural sunlight illuminates the front of his face while the back of his head remains in the shadows.

Ebenezer Hubbard (September 6, 1782–October 3, 1871)
Concord Public Library

On the list of sites to see in contemporary Concord, Massachusetts, is the statue commemorating the legendary minutemen present at the Battle of Lexington and Concord on April 19, 1775. If it weren't for the efforts of Ebenezer Hubbard, it is possible that this monument would not exist.

This son of Revolutionary War veteran David Hubbard and Mary Barrett was born in New Hampshire on September 6, 1782, but came to live in Concord with his grandfather and namesake at the age of ten. It's unclear why this move occurred. Perhaps his grandfather needed help on the farm, or possibly it was because Hubbard's father had died. His mother married for a second time in 1800. Whatever the reason, Hubbard eventually inherited his grandfather's farm and stayed in the town for the remainder of his days, living out his life as a bachelor.

In 1870, at the age of eighty, Hubbard posed for this carte de visite in a jacket, vest, and tie, his hair still wavy and plentiful. Hubbard died on October 3, 1871. He left the town one thousand dollars to commission a statue to men like his father who had fought in the first battle of the American Revolution. If the town did not comply, he left instructions that the money should be given to his birthplace of Hancock, New Hampshire.

The officials of the town of Concord moved to hire local artist and nationally known sculptor Daniel Chester French to design the statue and had it cast in bronze at the Ames Foundry in Chicopee, Massachusetts. The twenty-two-year-old Frenchman intended to portray Capt. Isaac Davis of Acton, who died at the battle. Since there were no portraits of Davis, he relied on paintings and family members as models. The finished statue features a man holding a musket standing next to a plow, conveying the fact that these first soldiers were farmers. As Hubbard had demanded, it was unveiled as part of the centennial celebration in April 1875.

Another Concord resident, Ralph Waldo Emerson, immortalized the battle in his poem "Concord Hymn," which begins, "By the rude bridge that arched the flood . . ." Today visitors to the area can stop at the monument of the minuteman and contemplate the Revolution.

Agrippa Hull (May 13, 1759–May 21, 1848)
Portrait taken from a daguerreotype at the Historical Collection of the Stockbridge Library Historical Collection

"It is not the cover of the book, but what the book contains . . . many a good book has dark covers" (Jones, *Stockbridge, Past and Present,* 242). Agrippa Hull, a Revolutionary War veteran, once remarked in a metaphor about race, not books. Hull, known as Grippy, was a celebrity in his native Stockbridge, Massachusetts, well known for his intelligence, witticisms, and quirkiness. He is one of the best-known African American figures of the American Revolution.

Born in 1759 in Northampton, Hull was brought to Stockbridge by Joab, a former servant of the religious revivalist Jonathan Edwards. Relatively little is known about his life until the American Revolution. When his mother married a second time, Hull supposedly didn't like his stepfather and chose to enlist in the cause for American liberty, saying that the "war could not last too long for him" (Jones, *Stockbridge, Past and Present,* 240).

He joined the Colonial army as a free-born black in 1777 at the age of eighteen, for the duration. In his case, it was for more than six years of continuous military service. His first duties as a "servant," or orderly, to Gen. John Paterson of the Massachusetts Line lasted for two years. For the remaining four years two months of service he fulfilled the same role for Polish soldier Gen. Thaddeus Kosciuszko, accompanying both commanding officers to military actions throughout the colonies.

Hull first applied for a pension under the Act of 1818. A reverent patriot, Hull didn't want to turn in his original discharge papers in support of his pension application because it contained George Washington's signature. In 1828, Charles Sedgwick, a local lawyer who was also Massachusetts Speaker of the House of Representatives, wrote letters of support asking for Hull's pension without the signed documents, because "he had rather forego the pension than lose the discharge." Sedgwick's petition was successful.

After the war, Hull purchased property in Stockbridge, where he became a caterer. In his spare time, Hull worked on behalf of the African American community. Together with Judge Theodore Sedgwick, father of the man who helped him obtain his pension, they sought to free Jane Darby, a slave who sought refuge in Stockbridge. Darby later became Hull's first wife.

Stories about Hull remain popular even today, including a report of a conversation between Hull and his employer. On one occasion Hull accompanied his white employer to hear a "distinguished mulatto preacher." Afterward the man asked Hull, "Well, how do you like nigger preaching?" to which Hull replied, "Sir, he was half black and half white. I like my half, how did you like yours?" (Jones, *Stockbridge, Past and Present,* 242). Another tale relates how Hull, who was in charge of Commander Kosciuszko's uniform, once wore the general's attire impersonating him at a dinner party for all the servants in camp. Kosciuszko returned to camp and discovered the charade.

This painting of Agrippa Hull at eighty-five years of age is in the Stockbridge Library Historical Collection in Stockbridge, Massachusetts. It is a copy of a daguerreotype done by Anson Clark in 1844. On the reverse is a note from Clark's journal: "Col. Dwight came with Agrippa Hull to have his 'Hull's' likeness taken & agreed to pay for it the next time he came over."

Margaret Timbrooke Hull (1782–April 12, 1870)
Historical Collection of the Stockbridge Library Association

After Agrippa Hull's death at the age of eighty-nine, his second wife, Margaret Timbrooke, applied for and received a widow's pension. Peggy married Hull on February 14, 1813. She came to Stockbridge at the age of eighteen from Great Barrington, Massachusetts.

The couple worked catering events of wealthy Stockbridge families, who held them in high regard as pious members of the community. Peggy had a reputation for making scrumptious gingerbread and root beer. The Hulls reportedly interacted with the entire town regardless of race, and they attended the Congregational Church.

When Margaret died in 1870, a newspaper notice proclaimed that "she was one of the best women that ever lived" (*Pittsfield Sun,* May 26, 1870). She left her possessions to their adopted daughter, Mary Gunn, who was by then known as Mrs. Way. A eulogy in the *Gleaner and Advocate* of Lee, Massachusetts, concluded, "Not far from 90 years had left their infirmities on her wasted frame, but had seemingly ripened her for the better land, where all souls are white in the same garments of imputed righteousness."

This carte de visite was taken in the late 1860s. In her hands she holds either a Bible or the daguerreotype of her late husband.

William Hutchings (October 6, 1764–May 2, 1866)
Reverend E. B. Hillard, The Last Men of the Revolution

Hutchings was another of Hillard's last men, but one who saw limited service. He was born in York, Maine, in what was then Massachusetts, to Charles Hutchings and Mary Perkins. In his pension application he claimed to be born in 1764 but lacked proof.

A biography of Hutchings by Joseph Williamson in *The American Historical Record* relates that in 1779, his family and the other inhabitants of the area around Castine, Maine, were forced to assist the British in the construction of the defenses at Fort George. When the British destroyed the American fleet, Hutchings's father refused to swear an oath of allegiance to Britain and moved his family to Newcastle.

Hutchings enlisted at the age of fifteen at Newcastle in 1781, serving as a private in Capt. Benjamin Lemont's Company, Col. Samuel McCobb's Massachusetts Militia, for six and a half months. He was taken prisoner at the Battle of Castine, Maine, while his unit tried to defend the coastline around the town. In Hillard's account, Hutching related how the British released him because of his young age.

Hutchings first applied for a pension in September 1832. Under that legislation, a veteran needed to prove at least six months of service. His father testified on his behalf, acknowledging his son's military service. In 1855, Hutchings applied for his bounty land allotment of 160 acres. He was also recognized for his service under the Special Act of 1865, which aided those pensioners still living.

After the war he remained in Maine, working as a farmer, a lumberman, and a mariner. Hillard remarked, "He smokes regularly, and uses spirituous liquors moderately. His mind is still vigorous, though his body is feeble" (*Last Men,* 82). By the time of Hillard's interview during the Civil War, Hutchings had lost several grandchildren in the conflict.

On July 4, 1865, he was a guest at an anniversary celebration for the Declaration of Independence. "A revenue cutter was detailed for his conveyance, and as he passed up the Penobscot River, the guns of Fort Knox fired a salute of welcome. The ovation, which was bestowed on the occasion, exceeded that ever before given to any person in the State" (*American Historical Record,* 243). Hutchings died May 7, 1867, at 102 years of age. He was the last living Revolutionary Veteran in New England. His final request involved the flag he'd fought to defend. He wanted it placed on his casket and unfurled at his burial.

The dark marks in this photo are stains from the glue used to adhere the photo to the card stock.

Andrew Jackson (1767–June 1845)
Library of Congress

Before he was president, this man of the people was a South Carolina boy whose Revolutionary fervor led him to enlist as a thirteen-year-old. Biographers describe his youthful character as impulsive, reckless, daring, and difficult to get along with. On May 12, 1780, Charlestown, South Carolina, fell to the British, leaving the area defenseless. In this atmosphere of fear of both British troops and the actions of the area's Tories, Elizabeth Jackson encouraged her younger sons to participate in militia drills and to prepare to fight the British. The war was real to the Jackson family; they'd already lost one son to the conflict.

Jackson's first field experience was at the Battle of Hanging Rock, serving with Col. William Richardson Davie. Later, back at their place of residence, the Waxhaw Settlement, Andrew and his brother Robert became guards for a military officer's house and soon were taken prisoner. Confronted by a British officer who requested that Jackson clean his boots, Jackson refused, supposedly declaring, "Sir, I am a prisoner of war, and claim to be treated as such" (Remini, *Andrew Jackson,* 21). In response, the officer aimed for Jackson's head with his sword while Jackson tried to block the hit with his left arm. He received gashes on his head and fingers that left permanent scars. His brother Robert received a similar blow, which would eventually be the cause of his death.

The boys, along with other captives, ended up in prison in Camden, New Jersey, without medical care, food, or bedding. Elizabeth Jackson interceded on their behalf and, with military support, helped get her starving sons and five neighbors released in exchange for fourteen British prisoners held by the Americans. As a result of their imprisonment, Jackson and his brother contracted smallpox and wound infections. Robert died soon after returning home. Andrew was ill for months, but the final blow of the Revolution for the Jackson family was about to occur. When Elizabeth left him to care for ill prisoners on a ship, she contracted cholera and subsequently died.

This print was engraved for the *Democratic Review* from a daguerreotype by Anthony, Edward and Co. taken on April 15, 1845. It is titled "In His Last Days." Another stoic daguerreotype, also pictured here, is associated with his presidency: it shows the strength of character he developed during his first military campaign, long before his heroic exploits during the War of 1812. Jackson's later life in politics was heavily influenced by the experience and military prowess he had forged as a child of the American Revolution.

David Kinnison
aged 102 yrs.

David Kinnison (?–February 24, 1852)
Stephan Lowentheil, New York City

Did he or didn't he? Kinnison's life is a combination of fact and fiction. Kinnison claimed to be present at both the Boston Massacre and the Boston Tea Party as well as having served in the military during the War of 1812. This famous last man supposedly lived to the age of 115 in Chicago, dying in 1852. He received a pension for his service, appeared in Benjamin Lossing's *Field-Book of the Revolution,* and had a monument erected to his memory. While the majority of writers replay his claims, the facts of his life bring questions to his story.

There is no doubt that Kinnison wove a believable tale of patriotic service and lived his later years as an icon of the Revolution. But there are discrepancies. During his interview with Lossing, he mentioned trying to enlist in Massachusetts in 1781 but was rejected because of his height: four foot nine inches. He gave his age as seventeen, which meant he was born in 1764, but it's likely that he was younger. Yet his pension file states that he "enlisted in March 1780 in Captain John Gooden's company[,] marched to West Point where he was put into Captain Sewell's company, Colonel Sprout's 2nd Massachusetts regiment[,] and served until summer or fall 1783." Kinnison claimed to be a veteran of both the American Revolution and the War of 1812.

Kinnison first applied for a pension for his service in the War of 1812 for which he received an annual sum of forty dollars and 160 acres of land when he qualified as an invalid—he had received an injury that contracted two fingers and affected his thumb.

In his Revolutionary War pension file, Kinnison claimed to be a variety of ages. In 1818, Kinnison, age fifty-six, renounced the War of 1812 pension to apply under the new statute for Revolutionary War veterans. At that time he related that he'd served for three years, from 1780 to 1783. In 1820 he filed an affidavit that he was seventy-nine, providing no explanation for the age difference. In the latter application, he said that his wife had died, leaving him with the care of four minor children. A timeline of Kinnison's life suggests that the truth of his military service is far from clear.

Whatever the true facts of Kinnison's life, he was lauded as the last survivor of the Boston Tea Party. An article about him appeared in *Harper's Magazine* in the early 1850s and catapulted him to national fame. His presence was commanded at banquets, parades, and events in his city of residence, Chicago. At the time of his death, his contemporaries believed him to be 115.

In this daguerreotype, Kinnison looks younger than either of his supposed ages. He has a full head of hair that actually looks like a mix of gray and natural hair color. His jaunty striped vest, offset by a loosely tied black silk tie, is paired with a jacket with prominent buttons. The photographer posed him seated next to a table. He appears younger here than in the commonly seen daguerreotype of him posed with a walking stick taken by Polycarpus Von Scheidau in Chicago in 1848. That image is in a private collection but was featured in *Facing the Light: Historic American Portrait Daguerreotypes.*

John Kitts (1762—September 1870)
Collection of Chester Urban

The printed caption on the front of this small card photograph reads, "John Kitts, aged 108 years old, The Last Revolutionary War Soldier," while on the back is the imprint for Norval H. Busey, 46 North Charles St., and in handwriting is "1869, Baltimore, U.S.A."

It's simultaneously a charming and sad picture of an elderly man with few teeth in a military uniform and a dirty tricorn hat, a gold watch draped around his neck. In the Federal Census of 1870, John Kitts, aged 108, of Baltimore, Maryland, listed his birthplace as Pennsylvania and his occupation as a marble finisher. At that time he was living with an African American domestic servant. This would establish his birth year as 1762.

This could be the same John Kitts who appears in an affidavit from 1782 in Thomas Dring's *Recollections of the Jersey Prison Ship.* This Kitts identified himself as "John Kitts of the city of Philadelphia, late mate of the sloop industry, commanded by Robert Harris." His testimony was given concerning a Captain Harris who issued a report on the condition of prisoners on the *Jersey.*

There is no record of Kitts requesting a pension for services; however, there is a rejected pension file for him. A letter in the file states that Kitts "presented to the House of Representatives a claim for Revolutionary War pension in the 41st Congress, 2nd and 3rd Sessions [1870]" (Pension Records). His action was recorded in the House Journal and his papers forwarded to the Committee on Revolutionary War Pensions. His pension claim was tabled with no further action. A year prior to his appeal to Congress, Kitts sought a local solution to his search for support. On October 21, 1869, a small news item appeared in the *New Hampshire Sentinel:* "John Kitts, aged 107, has presented a petition to the Baltimore City Council for aid for services rendered in the Revolutionary war and in 1812." It is likely that this news influenced his obtaining an invitation to visit President Ulysses S. Grant at the White House a few months later. This time the *Georgia Weekly Telegraph* picked up the story. According to the article, Kitt "alluded to the fact that he had met every President of the United States; that he witnessed the surrender of Lord Cornwallis at Yorktown and that he could not hope to survive another Presidential campaign, and while his memory served him he had called to pay his farewell regards to the Chief Magistrate of the nation, in the independence of which he had fought, and whose glory remained undimmed."

When he died in September 1870, his death notice claimed that he was a teamster for the army during the Revolutionary War. Whatever his role in the rebellion—soldier or sailor—Kitts outlived all other claimants, such as Daniel Bakeman and John Grey of Ohio. It appears he really was the Last Man of the Revolution (but one without official recognition or pension).

JOHN KITTS,
Norval H. Busey,
46 N. Charles Street.
Aged 108 Years. The Last Revolutionary Soldier.

Uzal Knapp (May 1758–January 10, 1856)
Collection of the New-York Historical Society

Photography has always been used as a copy medium, as evidenced by this daguerreotype duplicate of a painting of Uzal Knapp. Filed with the image is a note that states that daguerreotypist D. Esterly of Newburgh, New York, took this picture and gave it to the New-York Historical Society. At the time of the note, December 1, 1847, Knapp was still living in Montgomery, New York.

Knapp was born in Stamford, Connecticut, and enlisted in the army in 1777 for the duration of the war. Like other claimants, Knapp said he was with Washington's Life Guard serving as a sergeant. In his obituary in the *Daily Ohio Statesman,* it was reported that in 1780 he became part of the temporary increase of Washington's guards, serving in that capacity for two years. The Life Guard, also known as the Commander in Chief's Guard, was first organized in 1776 and remained in force until 1783 when only 86 men remained. In 1780 approximately 70 men were added to the unit, increasing its size from 180 to 250 men. According to Lossing, these men were chosen because of their "physical, moral and intellectual character."

Knapp's pension papers show that he served as a private in Capt. Stephen Betts's Company, 2nd Brigade of Connecticut Infantry, in 1777; was promoted to corporal in the same company; and was then made a sergeant on March 1, 1781. He stated that he was at the battles of White Marsh and Monmouth and was one of the soldiers to spend the winter at Valley Forge. He was discharged at West Point on June 1783 after six years of service. Washington's signature appears on his discharge papers.

Lossing visited Knapp and profiled him in his *Field-Book of the Revolution* and in other volumes he wrote about the patriots. At the time of their interview in the late 1840s, Lossing found Knapp fragile. Despite his frail condition, Knapp lived until 1856.

John Langdon (September 30, 1754–November 26, 1848)
New England Historic Genealogical Society

In 1842, John Langdon appeared in Suffolk County, Massachusetts, court to file legal documents in order to transfer his pension to Boston where he was residing with his daughter. Born at Hempstead, Queens County, in New York on September 30, 1754, he married Phebe Seaman of Dutchess County in 1778.

According to his pension statements, Langdon said he volunteered in June 1775 at the age of twenty-two for a company from North Hempstead. He also stated that he was in New York when the British, under General Howe's command, landed in Long Island in August 1776. He remarked that he "was a sergeant of the guard at DeLancy's Old Mansion in the Bowery where there was a prisoner, one of the desperadoes who murdered the Brother of Genl. Parfous, & whose watch was found upon him" (Pension Records). He survived yellow fever in August 1776. In September, after being released from a physician's care, Langdon boarded a sloop and was subsequently taken prisoner by the British at Long Island. He eventually escaped captivity in June 1777. Later that summer Langdon was at Saratoga with General Gates for General Burgoyne's surrender.

In his pension application, several fellow soldiers gave depositions in support of his application. One man claimed that he had known Langdon in 1778–80 and "that he was a warm and active man in the cause of his country and always sustained an excellent character for integrity and patriotism." When asked about additional service after 1777, Langdon couldn't recall all the details "in consequence of the great length of time which has elapsed since his revolutionary services and by reason of his age and the consequent loss of memory."

Langdon kept a diary of the last year of his life, recording an account of his descendants: "We [Langdon and his wife, Phebe] have been blessed with Ten children, Five Sons and Five Daughters." He goes on to name each one and provide details of their lives. In his early nineties and obviously thinking about his advanced age, Langdon also kept a list of local individuals living or recently deceased who were over ninety years of age. This daguerreotype was taken when he was ninety.

He died at the age of ninety-four. His obituary in the *Boston Daily Evening Transcript* stated that he was a member of the Society of Friends.

Enoch Leathers (October 2, 1763–May 28, 1858)
Historical Collections of Piscataquis County

This veteran of both the American Revolution and the War of 1812 was born in Dover, New Hampshire, and ended his days in Sangerville, Maine. Leathers enlisted for the Continental Army in June 1782, serving with Capt. Samuel Cherry, Col. George Reid's New Hampshire Battalion, for approximately two years. At the time of his pension claim in 1818 he was unsure of the length of his service but recalled that he was discharged at West Point. In his petition for a pension, he stated, "I am now under reduced circumstances & need the assistance of my Country for support" (Pension Records). Like many of the veterans, Leathers felt that he deserved some financial help in exchange for being in the armed forces during the Revolution. He began receiving a pension in September 1819.

After the Revolutionary War, he married Mary Cilley, had children, and settled in several small towns along the Maine frontier. The War of 1812 provided Leathers with another opportunity to fight for the United States. He enlisted in Captain Vose's Company in Colonel Ripley's Regiment. A transcription of his obituary appears in a history of Piscataquis County, Maine. It credits Leathers with a disregard for war, saying that, during a battle in the War of 1812, "he fired forty-four rounds, and how many proved fatal he did not know, but he prayed that God would save him from any more battles, and his prayer was answered." He spent the rest of the war guarding frontier residents from Indian attack. He received 160 acres for his War of 1812 service.

It is unknown when or where this daguerreotype was taken; in fact, the location of the original is unknown. Leathers died at the age of ninety-four, and it's likely that this image depicts him toward the end of his life. He looks at the camera through half-open eyes and holds what looks to be a handcrafted cane in clasped hands.

Dr. Howard
1845

Dr. Jonathan Leonard (February 17, 1763–January 25, 1849)
Private Collection

The American Revolution drove men's political passions and inspired them to make life-changing decisions, on both sides of the conflict. Jonathan Leonard, born in Bridgewater, Massachusetts, to Jonathan Leonard and Martha Washburn, was still in his teens when his Tory politics compelled him to leave the colonies. He eventually ended up in Bermuda, where he spent the last years of the war. Evidence of his residence on the island is a hand-sketched and signed map of the island that reads, "Jonathan Leonard fecit 1783." He left Bermuda shortly thereafter to attend Harvard University, from which he graduated in 1786. He received an honorary medical degree from Harvard in 1824.

Leonard studied with Dr. Wales, a physician and surgeon in Randolph, Massachusetts, before settling in Bridgewater and later Sandwich, Massachusetts. He married Temperance Hall, whom he met while boarding with her family. According to his obituary in the *Sandwich Observer* (January 1849), "Dr. Leonard was particularly happy in his domestic relation. For fifty years he lived with a devoted and affectionate wife." As a public testimony to his personality, the obituary also remarked that "at Dr. Leonard's fireside every man's character was safe."

In this portrait, probably taken shortly before his death, Leonard is wearing a cape and a single-breasted trimmed vest and carrying a cane. His formal attire suggests his prominent position within the community. A painted portrait of Dr. Leonard by an unknown artist also exists. On the reverse of the painting is written, "This portrait of Jonathan Leonard M.D. aged 70 was presented to him as a tribute of respect by the Ladies of Sandwich 1833." It is in private hands.

Morgan Lewis (October 16, 1754–April 7, 1844)
New York Public Library

A veteran of both the American Revolution and the War of 1812, this native of New York City and Princeton graduate was also the fourth governor of the state of New York. His father, Francis Lewis, a Welsh immigrant, was one of the signers of the Declaration of Independence.

Like so many young men of his generation, Lewis enlisted in June 1775, serving as a volunteer rifleman with a Pennsylvania unit. In August, the Provincial Congress directed the company he commanded to guard civilians removing arms from the Battery in New York while a British ship was at anchor nearby. Within a short time the ship began firing on the arsenal, and Lewis's men returned fire.

In November of that year, he served with the 2nd New York Continentals, which was eventually under his command as a major, as the original commander never assumed his duties.

In 1776, Lewis was promoted to colonel and acted as chief of staff to Gen. Horatio Gates in the Ticonderoga campaign, and Congress appointed him quartermaster general. Gates gave an order in September 1777 that "in the event of another conflict with the enemy, all orders given on the field by the adjutant, or quarter-master-general, are to be considered as coming from head quarters and to be obeyed accordingly" (Herring and Longacre, *National Portrait Gallery of Distinguished Americans with Biographical Sketches,* 2).

The following year, Colonel Lewis and General Clinton fought British regulars and General Brandt's Indian troops, which probably included Nikonah and Chainbreaker, two other men depicted in this book. In 1780, Lewis was with Clinton at the action at Crown Point along Lake Champlain. After the war, Lewis was colonel commandant in charge of the volunteer militia for New York City. In that capacity he escorted George Washington at his inauguration in 1789.

By that time Lewis had completed his legal studies and was a member of the New York Assembly and Senate. A series of appointments followed, including New York State attorney general and justice and chief justice of the New York Supreme Court. He was voted in as governor in 1804 and remained in office until 1807. Lewis supported schooling for all, declaring that "literary information should be placed within the reach of every description of citizen" (Herring and Longacre, *National Portrait Gallery of Distinguished Americans with Biographical Sketches,* 4). Through his military field experience he sought to improve the militia, and according to his biography by his granddaughter, Julia Delafield, he was responsible for adding the horse artillery.

When war loomed in 1812, Lewis was commissioned brigadier and quartermaster general for the U.S. Army. He was instrumental in gaining the release of prisoners of war using his own finances and reputation. It's estimated that he gave more than fourteen thousand dollars to accomplish the task. In 1813 he became a major general on the Niagara frontier.

In his sixties, Lewis directed his attention elsewhere. He helped establish New York University, was president of the New-York Historical Society (1832–36), and was president general of the Society of the Cincinnati (1839–44).

This engraving appeared in *Memoir, prepared at the request of a committee of the Common Council of the city of New York, and presented to the Mayor of the city, at the celebration of the completion of the New York Canals* as an extra illustration. It's based on a daguerreotype of Lewis taken by Howard Chilton.

Adam Link (November 14, 1761–August 15, 1864)
Reverend E. B. Hillard, The Last Men of the Revolution

His name appears on many of the lists of the "last men" and as such is profiled in Hillard's book on those men. According to Hillard, however, Link's military service in the American Revolution was "unimportant." In his pension application Link notes that he enlisted in 1777 at age seventeen in Wheeling, Virginia (in what today is West Virginia), and served in a variety of Pennsylvania units for a total of five years on the western frontier. He spent several short terms, from three to six months each, in different units, until his final tour from June to December 1779. Each time he was verbally discharged and thus lacked any written proof of his service for a pension application. He was a soldier for eighteen months all together.

In his 1833 pension application he declared, "I, Adam Link, applicant for a pension who has subscribed and sworn to the annexed declaration further state that in the war of the revolution my parents resided in Washington county in Pennsylvania near the line the State of Virginia, that our family suffered severely in the War, that the Indians murdered and scalped my father in the war, burnt his house and barn and took away all his stock of cattle and horse, and forced my father and family to leave their home with all the corn and crops standing on the land." Link's father was killed defending his property against the Indians in 1780.

According to Hillard, Link walked from Pennsylvania to Ohio at sixty years of age and at seventy cleared the land for a farm. This poor, hardworking man first received a pension in 1833 and then applied for bounty land at the age of ninety-two in 1855, receiving 160 acres. He died at the age of 102.

In this photograph, Hillard's photographer posed him in a rocking chair. With his cane held across his lap and his coat disheveled, Link looks in good health but tired.

Dolley (Payne) Madison (May 20, 1768–July 12, 1849)
Collections of the Maine Historical Society
Dolley Madison on the South Portico of the White House with President James Polk. Courtesy of the George Eastman House International Museum of Photography

Because no letters or diaries from her youth exist, all that is known of Dolley Payne's early years are anecdotal accounts from family and friends. Born May 20, 1768, into the Quaker community of New Garden, North Carolina, her birth is recorded in the monthly meeting records. Her parents, John and Mary Coles Payne, moved to North Carolina from Virginia and stayed for a little more than three years, then returned to their home state to live on their cousin Patrick Henry's Scotchtown Plantation. An uncredited biographer described her "laughing Irish eyes, her heavy eyebrows and long lashes, her black curling hair [and] brilliancy of her skin" (Côté, *Strength and Honor,* 51).

The fashionable first lady of Washington probably grew up following the Society of Friends' rules for plain dress—a one-piece outfit and drab colors. Her niece, Mary Estelle Elizabeth Cutts, wrote two manuscripts about her aunt's life and reported that Dolley's paternal grandmother often presented her with family jewelry, which she couldn't wear in public. She attended a Quaker school in Virginia, and her education probably consisted of domestic arts, penmanship, reading, and arithmetic, as was common for girls at the time.

Dolley was eight years old when the Revolution began and in her midteens by the end of the war. During those years, Virginia Quakers remained neutral as conscientious objectors. However, Anglican Patrick Henry, Dolley's first cousin and governor of Virginia, sided with the patriots. His legislature called for all Quaker records to be seized and examined for evidence of treason within the membership. Cedar Creek monthly meeting records were kept for several months then returned to their clerk, Dolley's father, John

Payne. While nineteenth-century biographers wrote that John Payne was a Revolutionary War hero, as the clerk of his meeting it is unlikely that he served, and no documentation has been found to the contrary. He did, however, emancipate all of the family's slaves within six months after the signing of the Declaration of Independence.

In 1790, Dolley married Quaker John Todd in Philadelphia. During the yellow fever epidemic of 1793, Dolley lost her in-laws, her son William, and her husband. After her husband's death that October, she and her young son, John Payne Todd, went to live with her mother in the family home in Philadelphia, which had become a boardinghouse for politicians and officials. In September 1794, the young widow married James Madison, a man seventeen years her senior.

Once her husband became secretary of state under Thomas Jefferson, Dolley became the official hostess of Washington and unofficial first lady, as both Jefferson and Vice President Aaron Burr were widowers. Friends wrote that her favorite pastimes were card games such as poker and snuff and that she loved fine clothes. But she wasn't focused on only socializing and frivolity: When the British burned Washington, D.C., during the War of 1812, she saved historic documents and paintings before fleeing herself.

Years later, after her husband's death in 1836, the impoverished Dolley returned to Washington and continued to be a social fixture, opening her house on New Year's Day and the Fourth of July. Her personality shines through in the iconic images of her as an elderly woman posed in her old-fashioned clothes and signature turban (fashionable during the War of 1812). In this daguerreotype, taken circa 1840, she wears a shawl made for her by a Maine woman, Julia Dearborn Wingate, whose husband was a protégé of Madison. The last image taken of Dolley Madison was a daguerreotype of her standing with a group, including President James K. Polk, on the South Portico of the White House in 1849. In the photograph are President and Mrs. James K. Polk, Secretary of State James Buchanan, Miss Payne, Miss Sarah Polk Rucker, Mr. Cave Johnson, Postmaster-General Judge John J. Mason, the Secretary of the Navy (either William Ballard Preston or John Y. Mason), Dolley Madison, Mrs. Cave Johnson, and an unidentified male. Dolley Madison died shortly after that image was taken.

John McCrillis (July 15, 1773–September 4, 1873)
Collection of David Allen Lambert

It is a childhood memory that connects McCrillis to the Revolution. While his native town of Nottingham, New Hampshire, wasn't the site of any battles, McCrillis's father and other men of the town participated in activities in support of independence. His early years made an impression on the young lad, and it's not difficult to imagine him playing soldier with his friends. He grew up in a house that was used as a tavern, a venue that also served as a meeting place in the eighteenth century. Wartime news would be spread by visitors stopping for the night or a pint, and certainly his father's adjoining blacksmith shop would be frequented by those traveling through the area.

A highlight of McCrillis's life was retelling his recollections of the American Revolution. He'd relate how he witnessed men enlisting in the army in exchange for a bounty of a two-year heifer and how at the end of the war he saw a cannon burst apart in a victory celebration.

McCrillis was an ordinary boy and a simple man. He trained as a blacksmith at his father's side and later took over the business. In 1796, his family moved to Goshen, New Hampshire, where McCrillis lived for the remainder of his life. Townspeople celebrated his one hundredth birthday by building a pavilion 120 feet long and 18 feet wide that was extended by 40-foot wings on either end. It was a daylong event featuring a brass band, fraternal brothers from neighboring towns, and elderly persons from the area. One of the highlights of the event was his son-in-law's reading of an account of McCrillis's life.

An elderly McCrillis sat for this small card photograph in the studio of J. Parker Jr. of Newport, New Hampshire. He looks contemplative and frail in this picture, leaning to one side with arms crossed. It's a dignified portrait of the man known as the "Blacksmith of Goshen."

Alexander Milliner (a.k.a. Alexander Maroney) (c. 1760–March 1865)
Reverend E. B. Hillard, The Last Men of the Revolution

The facts of Milliner's early life are confused. Milliner told Hillard he was born in Quebec in 1760, but his pension documents suggest that he was actually born circa 1770. Even his surname is uncertain; at times he was known as Milliner, and at others he adopted his stepfather's surname of Maroney. Hillard found him living in a little town called Adam's Basin, not far from Odgen, Monroe County, New York.

By the time Hillard interviewed him, Milliner's memory was not accurate. In his 1819 pension application, filed under the name Alexander Maroney, documents state that "his father Florence Maroney enlisted him as a drummer boy commanded by Capt. [John] Graham [2nd New York Regiment]" (Pension Records). Milliner told Hillard that he'd served in Gen. George Washington's Life Guards in that capacity, but he doesn't appear on any member roster of that unit.

In support of his claim to being one of the Life Guards, he told Hillard anecdotes about Washington. As they marched by a group of boys playing a game with stones, the general had them stop their game, saying, "Now, boys, I will show you how to jerk a stone" (*Last Men,* 71). Washington beat them all. To Hillard, Milliner professed to being present at numerous battles including Yorktown. He reminisced how General and Mrs. Washington often visited the troops, calling them their "boys."

Milliner served for six and a half years, part of the time in New York regiments, until being discharged in June 1783. Milliner told Hilliard that he joined the navy afterward, serving for five and a half years, including service in the War of 1812, but there was no documented evidence at the time to support this assertion.

As a recipient of a pension in 1818, he had to reapply in 1820, listing his personal property and answering questions about his financial worth. "Real Estate, I have none" (Pension Records). He did own one ox, as well as some miscellaneous household and farm implements. His dependents included a sickly wife and children. At the age of ninety-four in 1855 he applied for bounty land and received his 160 acres.

According to Hilliard, at the time of this photograph, Milliner played his drum for the photographer and sang. He died soon after, in March 1865.

Nikonah

American Philosophical Society

During the American Revolution, some Native American tribal leaders supported the British cause while others worked with the patriots. Familiar with the territory in their area, some native guides helped the army maneuver through terrain and acted as scouts seeking information on troop movements while others, like Nikonah, fought side by side with their allies. He was a member of the Tutelo tribe.

In 1763, the Tutelo, originally from North Carolina and Virginia, consisted of four small tribes that had a population of approximately a thousand people, including only two hundred men. At the time of the war, the tribal members resided near what is present-day Ithaca, New York.

During the American Revolution, the Tutelo, as members of the Six Nations, sided with the British. Nikonah served with British general Joseph Brant, chief of the Iroquois. Brandt and his Indian supporters ambushed Americans at Oriskany, New York, on August 6, 1777. It was a massacre, and Lossing, in his *Field-Book of the Revolution,* called it "the bloodiest battle of the war."

In 1779, American general John Sullivan destroyed the Tutelo town of Coreorgonel as retribution for the tribe's siding with the British. After the war, the United States government made the tribes that allied with their enemy move to Canada; a small group of Tutelo Indians still lives near Brantford, Ontario.

Almost a century later, with gnarled hands and wearing a British military coat, Nikonah smiled into the camera for ethnographer Horatio Hale in Ontario. At the time, Nikonah was the last living full-blooded member of his tribe. Hale visited Nikonah to hear him speak his native tongue so that Hale could study the linguistic roots of the tribe.

NIKONHA, THE LAST TUTELO.
IN 1870; AGED 106.

Tirzah (Whitney) Palmer (March 30, 1769–August 27, 1852/53
Collection of Joe Bauman

On the back of this daguerreotype is a handwritten note that begins, "Grandmother Palmer, died Spring of 1861 aged 94 years," followed by a list of three generations of direct descent through her son Timothy. It seems to outline the provenance of the object. It's this information that identifies her as Tirzah Palmer, widow of Revolutionary War veteran Noah Palmer. Their life history illustrates a country with a mobile population.

She was born in Montague, Massachusetts, while Noah was born February 9, 1756, in Nine Partners, New York. According to the genealogy of the Palmer family, he married first a Miss Southerland in 1776 and had four children. His first wife died in 1785. Two years later he married Tirzah, daughter of Ephraim and Rhoda Whitney. They had ten children born in Vermont and New York State.

Noah Palmer enlisted as a minuteman in Dutchess County, New York, in June 1775, serving for one year. He joined the Continental service on July 1, 1776, for six months, the longest of his stints in the military in a company that joined the regiment under the command of Gen. George Clinton at White Plains and Peekskill, New York. Palmer served in 1778 for three months and then for another month and twelve days. In 1779 he signed on for two terms of one month and twelve days each, the first as a volunteer with Captain Southerland "in pursuit of the Indians" (Pension Records). He reported in his pension claims that they didn't find any. He also claimed to have served in the late years of the war with Captain Tallmadge seeking Tories.

In his 1832 pension application, he stated that he hadn't served in any battles and that each time he had enlisted he was a private. His file outlines his multiple places of residence in New York. The longest was the twenty years he spent in Chenango County. He had no one that could vouch for his service and no discharge papers. A local minister came forward to support his age claim, because Palmer also lacked proof of his birth. His pension application was rejected, however. He could have been rejected for having less than six months' service under the 1832 act.

Almost two hundred years later, family historian Horace Wilbur Palmer found his birth date in a Palmer family Bible.

According to Ford L. Palmer, a descendant interviewed for the *Palmer Genealogy,* two of Noah's brothers moved to Canada as Tories, and he refused to ever visit them, although their children visited each other. It is this statement that suggests that Noah Palmer felt strongly about the Revolutionary ideals for which he fought.

This undated daguerreotype of Tirzah is slightly blurry due to her having moved while the picture was being taken. She wears a dark scarf over her steely gray hair underneath her day cap and looks nervous and uncertain about posing for the photographer. While little is known about her life, fifteen years after her husband's death in 1840, Tirzah Palmer applied for and received bounty land as allowed by the law for her husband's service. Tirzah qualified under the 1855 bounty land act, because it only required sixteen days' service or participation in any battle. She was eighty-seven years old and probably applied on behalf of one of her children. She died near Glen Falls, New York.

Thomas Handasyd Perkins (December 15, 1764–January 11, 1854)
Collection of the Boston Athenaeum

In this daguerreotype taken circa 1853, Thomas Handasyd Perkins sits in profile, his arm on an open book of what appears to be raised writing for the sightless. His milky eyes attest to his blindness. According to the cataloging record, this image is sealed in a passe-partout inside a double-elliptical frame of molded black thermoplastic over a wood core. The intricacy of the framed image is clearly an indication of his status and wealth.

Near the end of his life, this wealthy man had inherited a fortune and amassed one of his own as an international businessman. As an import-export merchant, he was involved in the China Trade—American products for tea. He was a member of the Boston Brahmin and came into contact with many of the great men of the Federalist period. At one point he brought the son of the Marquis de Lafayette to live with his godfather, George Washington. But for all his worldwide adventures, this Boston native never forgot the scenes he witnessed in Boston as a child.

In his early childhood, Boston was a city full of Revolutionary fervor, with John Adams at the forefront of the revolt against British rule and British regiments camped throughout the city. In March 1770 an increasing number of altercations occurred between the troops and the citizens. Name calling and physical incidents were not unusual. On the night of March 5, ringing church bells announced an alarm, and thinking it was a fire, both British troops and a mob of citizens gathered at King Street near the town pump at Jackson's Corner. It was a cold March day with snow on the ground from earlier storms. In a similar situation to what had transpired in past weeks, with taunts from the crowd angering the troops, this time it exploded into deadly violence. Men jeered at the soldiers and boys threw material onto the roof of the Custom House so that it would roll down on the soldiers. The crowd threw icy snowballs on the troops, who fired into the crowd, not with powder to simply scare them, but with live ammunition, killing several. Later in life Perkins remarked, "The impression made on my mind by the death scene, and the frozen blood in the street, was of course indelible and I now well remember the location of each body, although the houses where the bodies laid have long since been replaced by new stone edifices" (Seaburg and Patterson, *Merchant Prince of Boston,* 14).

Perkins's childhood in Boston must have been marked by other scenes of resistance and, eventually, war. Perkins's father, James Perkins, was a member of the Sons of Liberty, and it's likely that young Thomas heard his father talk about the activities of that group. When his father died in 1773, Thomas was nine. His mother, Elizabeth, supported the family by selling groceries, including tea at the time of the Boston Tea Party, an event that must have affected their finances. She evacuated her young children from Boston to Barnstable on Cape Cod before the Battle of Bunker Hill.

According to Perkins's biography, his mother let her sons train with guns in case they needed to join the cause. In 1776, Perkins and his family returned to Boston. He remembered hearing the reading of the Declaration of Independence at the Old State House on July 19.

After the war, he began his travels and the building of his successful business empire. Biographer Thomas G. Cary, in his memoir of Perkins published after the latter's death in 1854, wrote that he was the leading merchant in New England and a generous philanthropist. Perkins helped establish the Perkins School for the Blind. The raised writing in the photo could be Boston Line Type, an embossed alphabet developed by Samuel Gridley Howe, director of the Perkins School. Books of this font were produced until 1881. Perkins also promoted the building of the Bunker Hill Monument. He inspired the respect of contemporaries such as Daniel Webster, who in 1843 at the dedication ceremony for the monument said of Perkins, "His charities have distilled, like the dews of heaven; he has fed the hungry, and clothed the naked; he has given sight to the blind; and for such virtues there is a reward on high, of which all human memorials, all language of brass and stone, are but humble types and attempted imitations" (Webster, *Address Delivered at the Laying of the Cornerstone,* 6).

William Plumer (1759–1851)
New Hampshire Historical Society

Not every man or young man of age fought in the American Revolution. Plumer, the son of Samuel Plumer and Mary Dole, did not enlist in the militia. Neither Plumer nor his father were ardent patriots. According to law he should have enrolled in the military at the age of sixteen in 1775, but he didn't. He'd lived in Epping, New Hampshire, since the age of nine but didn't participate in the military support of the town even when the state legislature made it mandatory.

During the war, it was religion, not politics, that interested Plumer. He was deeply affected by the religious revivalism of local evangelist, Dr. Samuel Shepard. Plumer wrote about his conversion. Despite his lukewarm support for the Revolutionary cause, this self-taught man first spent time as an itinerant Baptist minister and then became involved in politics by writing articles for the *New Hampshire Gazette* on the state constitution's stand on religion. In 1787 he studied to become a lawyer and chose a career as a politician.

He served in the political arena as a Federalist in support of the Constitution first on the local level, as a town selectman and justice of the peace. In state affairs he served in the state legislature and in 1790–91 contributed so much to the revision of the New Hampshire State Constitution of 1784 that it became known as "Plumer's Constitution."

In 1802, now with a wife and children, Plumer became a United States senator, initially opposing Jefferson's agenda. When Jeffersonians began supporting Federalist principles, he sided with James Madison. He returned to the New Hampshire State Senate for two years, then became governor as a Democratic Republican in 1812; he returned to the senate with the elections of 1816–19.

His major contribution to American politics is his detailed record of all the debates held during his term in the United States Senate, including discussions on the Louisiana Purchase treaty. When President Thomas Jefferson assumed that the Senate would approve the measure, Plumer remarked that Jefferson was ignoring the Senate's "freedom of opinion." His three and a half years' worth of notes on Senate sessions provides a unique view of the workings of that body. His *Memorandum of the Proceedings of Congress, 1803–1807* wouldn't be published until the early twentieth century.

It is unknown when he sat for this daguerreotype, but its early style mat and unclear image suggest that it dates from the early 1840s. Here he sits with stooped posture in a sturdy wood chair wearing a light-colored coat and a serious expression. Plumer died in Epping at the age of ninety-two. He was the last living member of New Hampshire's Constitutional Convention.

Jeremiah Powell (February 15, 1750–August 29, 1852)
Courtesy of Richard Draves

At the beginning of the war, Powell volunteered for two short terms, first in Captain Boyd's Company and then in November 1775 as a substitute for a Nathaniel Scott, who'd only served half of his eight-month contract. In 1777, Powell was drafted for three months into Capt. Peter Penniman's Company, and they marched to Bennington, Vermont. In his pension application he stated that he'd been at the Battle of Saratoga with General Gage but was not "called into the heat of battle." His company was held back, waiting to be called and then remained at Bennington until they were discharged. In the fall of 1778 he remembered being at Smithfield, Rhode Island, in Captain Potter's Regiment as an orderly sergeant at Warwick Neck, one of the many fortifications protecting the strategic passages of Narragansett Bay.

According to his descendant, Richard Draves, Powell was born in Bellingham, Massachusetts, and after the war lived in Smithfield, Rhode Island, and then in New Hartford in Oneida, New York, with his wife, Elizabeth Sayles. There is no extant information on the parentage of either Jeremiah or Elizabeth. The couple had seven children, four born in Massachusetts and three in New York.

An account of his one hundredth birthday appeared in the *Oneida Morning Herald* of December 18, 1850, noting, "The white-haired man sat upon the platform, by the side of the preacher. He appeared remarkable vigorous [*sic*] and hale for one on his centenial [*sic*] birthday." Many of his descendants lived into their late eighties and nineties. This photograph is rumored to have been taken to commemorate his one hundredth birthday. It's a copy of a daguerreotype. The original is now lost. There are water stains along the bottom edge of the print. In this image, Powell wears a heavy coat and vest buttoned to the silk stock wrapped around his upturned collar. While he's bald on top, the white hair on the sides of his head is long enough to touch his collar. In his hand he carries a walking stick.

Roger Kingsley Powell, a descendant, and his wife, Doris Wilson Powell, wrote that Powell lived with his son, Liberty, and related that "family stories tell that Jeremiah was a hearty man and often walked five miles to visit his son Philo, and was active until the winter of 1852 when it is reported he slipped on the ice and fell, after casting his ballot in the local election."

Isaac Rice (October 14, 1765–August 11, 1852)
Illustration from Benjamin Lossing, Pictorial Field-Book of the Revolution

Drawn by the chance of pension money, land grants, and the glory of being an American patriot, some men posed as veterans while others who honorably served couldn't provide adequate documentation to prove their service. This lack of proof disqualified many individuals from receiving a pension and in other cases led to their being tossed off the rolls as imposters. When Isaac Rice took Benjamin Lossing, author of the *Pictorial Field-Book of the Revolution,* on a tour of Fort Ticonderoga, he claimed to be a veteran. This sketch of Rice was drawn during that visit. Rice spoke of his military service, stating that he "performed garrison duty at Ticonderoga under St. Clair, was in the field at Saratoga in 1777, and served a regular term in the army" but lacked the documentation to prove his service. Eighty-five at the time of Lossing's visit, Rice supported himself giving guided tours of the fort. In addition to his own noteworthy military career, he mentioned that his elder brother had served with Col. Ethan Allen of the Green Mountain Boys when they captured the fort from the British in 1775.

His was a romantic tale of two brothers and their association with two well-known Revolutionary War figures—Arthur St. Clair and Ethan Allen. Allen and Benedict Arnold captured the fort from the British in May 1775. Allen was commander of the Green Mountain Boys, a group formed during the territorial conflict between New York and New Hampshire over the area of Vermont before the Revolution. At several points during the early 1770s a sizable bounty was offered for Allen's capture. His unit was called to service when a force was needed to take Fort Ticonderoga from the British. Shortly after this successful campaign, he was voted out of command by his troops.

Arthur St. Clair, a Scottish immigrant and Continental general, had an impressive career in the colonial wars, serving in the British army in North America during the French and Indian War. Afterward he resigned, became an extensive landowner in Pennsylvania, then accepted a commission under Gen. George Washington in 1775. In 1777 he ordered the withdrawal of troops from Fort Ticonderoga during the beginning of the Saratoga campaign and for his actions was nearly court-martialed. While some thought his decision sound, others questioned his loyalty and thought him a traitor like Benedict Arnold. St. Clair would later become the only governor of the Northwest Territory.

Rice chose to link his service to two colorful characters—one dashing, the other suspicious. Whether Rice embellished his past for the sake of tourists or whether he actually participated as a soldier is still being debated. According to his death notice, Rice was buried on the grounds of the fort, as was his dying wish.

Chief Sopiel Selmore (March 1, 1814–1860)
Collections of the Maine Historical Society

During the Revolutionary War, members of various tribal nations fought on both sides of the conflict. In March 1775, the Stockbridge Indians formed a company of minutemen under the Massachusetts Provincial Congress. A few months later, the Continental Congress, in response to the formation of the Stockbridge Indian unit, told its Indian commissioners to either keep tribal members neutral or enlist them in the American effort.

One of these Native American groups was the Passamaquoddy, of the Algonquian-speaking tribes of the Abenaki Nation, who fought on the American side of the conflict. In 1610 it is estimated that only one thousand members lived near Pleasant Point on Passamaquoddy Bay in Maine and in New Brunswick. By 1800, fewer than two hundred remained in the area.

In 1895, Chief Sopiel Selmore, son of Capt. Selmore Soctomah and Dinnis Molly Selmore, applied for membership in the Maine Sons of the American Revolution (SAR). An 1860 interview with his one-hundred-year-old father served as his proof of service, thus allowing his son to join the SAR. Soctomah duly swore that when he was nineteen years of age, "he with fifty others of his tribe, took from the English in the time of the Revolution an armed schooner in Passamaquoddy Bay" (SAR), giving it to Col. John Allen. After this daring escapade, he volunteered for further service as an Indian scout for the Maine colonial militia under Allen at Potato Point in Machias, Maine. During the War of 1812, Soctomah served as a pilot and assisted troops under the command of Lt. Enoch Manning.

Soctomah remained friends with Allen even after the Revolution, a fact noted in Selmore's application. Allen's son John supported Soctomah's claim of military service through personal knowledge of his serving "under the command of his father, that he was certain for he recollected it, and had always known him" (SAR).

Selmore appears in the 1900 Federal Census of Maine in the special inquiry relating to Indians as eighty-nine years of age and living in the house he owned with his wife of fifty-one years, a son, a daughter and her husband, and several of their children. His wife gave birth to ten children but only five were still living at the time of census. Under occupation is "tribe—captain." He stated that both his parents were Passamaquoddy and that he was a full-blooded member of the tribe. Selmore was the only Native American member of the Maine SAR.

This hand-tinted portrait of Chief Selmore depicts him in ceremonial dress. It is unknown when it was taken.

Six Aged Citizens of Bennington
Bennington Museum, Bennington, Vermont
Samuel Fay (August 17, 1772–December 25, 1863)
Bennington Museum, Bennington, Vermont

This very faint daguerreotype is the only known group portrait of a gathering of last men. The occasion was the anniversary of the Battle of Bennington in 1848. All but one of these men was a child at the time of the Revolution, but several claimed to have fought beside their fathers, recollecting events of the days surrounding the skirmish. These are the faces of the sons of Ethan Allen's Green Mountain Boys.

Sitting (left to right) are Benjamin Harwood (1762–1851), Abisha Kingsley (1766–1859), Aaron Robinson (1768–1849), and Samuel Safford (1761–1851). Standing (left to right) is Capt. David Robinson (1777–1858) and Samuel Fay (1772–1863).

According to a family Bible purportedly owned by Stephen Fay of the Catamount Tavern, "This picture was taken in September 1848 of Samuel Safford, who was in the Battle of Bennington, and Samuel Fay, Abisha Kingsley, Aaron Robinson, David Robinson and Benjamin Harwood. Their united ages when the picture was taken was four hundred and eighty nine years old." Also included was a list of birth and death dates for each of the men in the picture.

In this image Harwood sits hunched over, holding a sword that likely belonged to his father. He is the most infirm of the group. Safford's father was a major in Allen's unit. In the family record it's noted that Samuel was the first man to "scale the Tory breastworks at the Battle."

Only Fay's obituary in a history of Bennington, Vermont, mentions his participation in the war. According to Fay, on his fifth birthday his father took him along to the Battle of Bennington, fought on August 16, 1777. His father ran the Catamount Tavern where the Green Mountain Boys were established. Built in 1769, it burned in 1871. A monument stands today on the original site. During the Revolution, tradition holds that Allen planned the Ticonderoga attack, and Stark plotted the surrender of Burgoyne while at the tavern.

In *Memorials of a Century,* the ninety-two-year-old Fay clearly recalled the events of that day—the sounds of the guns and the confusion.

(Possibly) David Smiley (April 10, 1760–October 3, 1855)
Collection of William Schaeffer

For every identified daguerreotype, there are several unidentified ones sitting in family collections and private archives. In the 1970s, William Schaeffer bought five unidentified daguerreotypes of the same man from an Andover, Massachusetts, dealer. Years later he also bought a carte de visite copy of one of them. The carte de visite has a photographer's imprint on the back—"Scriptures, 2 French's Block, Peterboro, N.H." So who is this man? It appears from the daguerreotypes that he's not poor and that he sat for a likeness every year or two for a decade. Possibly we can assume that he's from Peterboro, where the copy was made. This unidentified man began posing for portraits in the 1840s when daguerreotypists used simple pebbly textured mats and continued until at least the mid-1850s, as evidenced by the decorative mat on the last image of him. Through the sequential images he appears to age before our eyes.

Searching census records, pension applications, and local histories for men of means who lived into the age of photography in New Hampshire and would be the right age for this man, I uncovered several possibilities, but only one man lived long enough. Dr. David Smiley, born April 10, 1760, lived until October 3, 1855, when he died at the age of ninety-five. It's a tentative identification, but if Smiley sat for this many portraits, perhaps there is a captioned photograph of him in a family collection.

Smiley served two terms in the army in the American Revolution. He received a pension in 1818 for his time in the Continental troops. His 1820 pension application claims that he served for nine months in the Massachusetts Line and later as a guard in the Fishkill Mountains. He was struck from the rolls at that point, unable to show a familial need for a pension.

In the *History of Peterboro (New Hampshire)* it's reported that he remembered walking sixty miles in one day as a soldier and using all of his money to buy a day's worth of food. Although the town history and his obituary list him as a doctor, he clearly states in his pension that his occupation was "husbandman." In March 1855, he applied for bounty land as payment for his Revolutionary War service.

Isaac Snow (December 8, 1757–May 12, 1855)
Orleans Historical Society

Snow sat for this daguerreotype in 1852 at the age of ninety-four. It's a serious-looking portrait of a man who served in both the army and the navy during the American Revolution. In this distinguished portrait, Snow looks off into the distance, clutching an unidentified document. This is a copy of the original daguerreotype; the location of the actual image is unknown.

Born in the coastline village of Tonset (East Orleans), Massachusetts, this small-town man traveled far from home during the Revolutionary War and experienced the deprivations of a prisoner of war. Details of Snow's military service appear in his 1832 pension claim. He served for a short term of two months in early 1776 with Capt. Isaiah Higgins at Nantasket, Massachusetts, and then for another six months with the same commander. He appeared on the payroll of Capt. Benjamin Godfrey's Company in Col. Josiah Whitney's Regiment of Massachusetts militia for six months in 1777 and stated in his pension documents that he was with this unit at South Kingstown, Rhode Island.

According to his pension papers, he boarded the ship *Defense* in January 1778 when it was lengthened from a brig to a full-size ship commanded by Capt. Samuel Smedly of Connecticut. The ship traveled from the West India Islands to the banks off Newfoundland looking for British ships. Snow was one of the first American sailors vaccinated with live smallpox virus while aboard the *Defense*.

During his three years in the navy, Snow was taken prisoner twice. The first time, he managed to escape from a British prison ship moored near Lisbon, Portugal, walked to Brest, France, and found passage home with French troops coming to America to support the Revolution. His second capture in 1780 as an Admiralty prisoner of war landed him in Old Mill Prison in Plymouth, England, until a prisoner exchange in 1783.

After the war, Snow returned home and, along with other Revolutionary War veterans, was instrumental in naming Orleans in honor of French participation in the Revolution. During the War of 1812, he helped deflect a British landing at Rock Harbor (Orleans) in December 1814.

Snow held a variety of occupations, working as a builder, a miller of grain, and a cobbler before receiving his pension in 1832. At the time of his death, he held the distinction of being both the oldest living Revolutionary War veteran in Barnstable County and its oldest citizen.

Clark Stevens (October 15, 1764–November 1853)
Collection of the Boston Athenaeum

Stevens's hometown of Rochester, Massachusetts, sits on the southeastern coast of the state. Just prior to the American Revolution, the Rochester town meeting was concerned about the effects of a war on their town. In 1774, they proactively voted to choose officers who would train up to 100 minutemen for three half-days a week and "twice in a month in one Body to Learn the use of the Fire-Licks (muskets)" (*Mattapoisett and old Rochester, Massachusetts,* 128). Each man would have a firearm and the provisions as recommended by the provincial congress. For their efforts, each man received a shilling a week. Rochester sent three companies to fight in 1775 following the skirmish at Lexington and Concord. At eighteen, Stevens and his father, Prince, enlisted together to serve in a company of Rochester, Massachusetts, militia. One biography suggests that Clark was drafted. At the end of the war, Stevens left the army to become a sailor on a New Bedford whaler. It was an event that changed his life.

According to the *History of Montpelier,* he nearly drowned at sea and experienced so many traumatic events that, when he returned home, he moved to Montpelier, Vermont, far away from the ocean. Several members of his family followed him there. The time at sea inspired him to seek a quiet life and pursue religion.

It appears that, after the war, Stevens became a member of the Society of Friends, or Quakers, in Vermont. Stevens was an active member of the meeting at Montpelier, traveling to attend monthly, quarterly, and yearly meetings on behalf of his community. He actually built the log meeting house for use of the meeting. The Montpelier Meeting only lasted from 1798 to circa 1840.

A physical description of him appears in the *History of Montpelier:* "Full six feet high, and nobly proportioned, with a shapely contour of head and features, dark eyes and a sedate, thoughtful countenance, his presence was unusually imposing and dignified." All of these features are seen in this daguerreotype of Stevens posed with his Quaker hat on his head and his cane clasped in front of him. At some point around 1850, Stevens was in Boston on business and took a moment to have this likeness taken by Southworth and Hawes.

Looking at this image, it's not difficult to imagine that his dying words in 1853 were as reported: "I have endeavored to do what I apprehended was required of me. I have naught but feelings of love for all mankind; and my hope of salvation is based on the mercy of God through his Son, Jesus Christ" (Thompson, *History of the Town of Montpelier,* 180). Humble and intelligent, Stevens left his mark on those he met and helped.

Flora Stewart (d. 1868)
Collection of Greg French

A death notice for Stewart appeared in the *Farmer's Cabinet* on August 27, 1868. It proclaimed, "Mrs. Flora Stewart, the oldest person in New Hampshire, a colored woman who is said to have attained the great age of 103 years, died in Londonderry on Monday." Her age may have been off by more than a decade.

Just a year before, on May 23, 1867, a reporter for the *Manchester Mirror* interviewed her for a piece recording her remarkable life. According to the article, Stewart was a slave owned by the grandfather of Samuel Wilson Sim(p)son, whose mother Stewart nursed as a baby. The reporter wrote, "Flora is full of vim, with remarkable retentive memory." She described a dinner they had served in the residence in which she had been a house slave: "I made up thirty pounds of sugar with my own hands into cakes, and for dinner were killed cattle, turkeys, geese and chickens, and they had roast pigs, each with an ear of corn in his mouth."

At the time of the interview, the eighty-year-old Simpson claimed that he had proof that Stewart was at least 119 years old, stating that Flora was part of the household when his father was an infant in 1748. A subsequent story was reported to have appeared in the *Manchester American,* stating that Stewart claimed she was the oldest person known in the United States and that she had been born in Boston in 1750. She told the second correspondent that her family came to live with the Simpsons as slaves when she was three months old and remained in their employ after the abolition of slavery. A history of Candia, a town in which she lived for a few years, claimed she was owned by the Wilson family and took that as her surname.

During the Revolutionary period, slavery was a much debated topic in New Hampshire. As of 1773 there were 646 slaves, including Stewart and her parents. A decade later the number had dropped to fewer than fifty. Prince Whipple, a slave owned by a New Hampshire Continental Army officer, and eighteen other blacks wrote to the legislature seeking their freedom. They phrased their document using words such as *justice* and *rights of man.* Nothing happened. It wasn't until 1783 that the state constitution proclaimed that "all men are born equal and independent." There were still 158 slaves in the 1790 state census, but only eight in 1800. The official end to slavery in the state is 1857, just a few years before the passage of the federal Emancipation Proclamation. Unlike slaves in Southern states, New Hampshire blacks were allowed to vote in the election of 1860. It's unknown whether Stewart was freed or remained a slave into the nineteenth century.

Regarding this picture of her, another article published in 1867 stated "that she was at Manchester on Wednesday and had photographs of herself taken, and was very much surprised at the process" (*Lowell Daily Citizen and News*). The printed caption on the front of this carte de visite states her age as 117 and the date taken as November 5, 1867. She dressed for her portrait in formal long black gloves and a dark-colored dress and cape. She has wrapped her head in a scarf. It's not her clothes but the pose that is striking. Her direct gaze and erect posture in the carved chair give her a regal look, her cane reminiscent of a scepter. When she died in 1868, most of the townspeople of Londonderry were reportedly in attendance at her funeral.

FLORA STEWART, LONDONDERRY, N. H.
Aged 117 years. Taken Nov. 5, 1867.

Jabez Huntington Tomlinson (December 1760–January 14, 1849)
Yale University

It was a single event during the American Revolution that inspired Tomlinson to enlist. In early June 1779, while a junior at Yale College, now Yale University, Tomlinson spent the night with the Lewis family. At the time he was engaged to their daughter Rebecca. During the night, the British raided the home, took the family's belongings, and imprisoned Tomlinson. They were acting on a tip that there was support for the Revolution at the college. An account of the noteworthy event was in the New Haven *Journal* of June 9, 1779: "One night last week a party from L. I. [Long Island] landed at Old Mill in Stratford, and plundered the house of Mr. Joseph Lewis of a considerable sum of money, all the clothing, linen, etc and went off with their booty, taking with them a young man named Tomlinson, a member of Yale College, who was there on a visit."

More specific details appeared in a history of Stratford written by a Mrs. Rufus W. Bunnell. She recalled, "The soldiers not only stripped the house of all supplies of food stored for the winter, but, taking the quilts and coverings from the beds, spread them on the floor and emptied into them the contents of all the drawers and chests and even the wearing apparel in daily use, tied them and carried all away" (Wilcoxson, *History of Stratford, Connecticut,* 517). The men also found a stash of Continental currency, which they took as well.

As far as her memories of Tomlinson's capture, Bunnell recollected that he was made to dress, taken to Long Island and then to New York's infamous Sugar House Prison. Tomlinson supposedly wrote to British general Henry Clinton, asking for release. Bunnell remembered hearing that Clinton actually interviewed Tomlinson before he released him.

Tomlinson, the son of Capt. Gideon Tomlinson and Hannah Huntington, became an orphan at five and resided with his paternal grandfather until he was eight, when his care was turned over to a family friend, the Reverend Izrahiah Wetmore. He married Rebecca Lewis in January 1780 while he was still a student. After she died on January 1, 1823, he married Phebe Birdseye on December 12, 1849.

Just a year after his imprisonment, in April 1780, Tomlinson was an ensign in Capt. John Riley's Company in Col. S. B. Webb's Continental regiment charged with guarding British major and spy John André, who was involved in Benedict Arnold's treasonous activities. André had been Clinton's aide dealing with correspondence relating to spying. This led him to meet with Arnold to discuss plans to assist the British. Arnold sent information to André through an intermediary. This eventually led to André's capture and execution.

Shortly before he was hung, André presented Tomlinson with a charcoal sketch of himself, which is now in the collection of Yale University.

Tomlinson stayed in the service until May 1, 1781. He graduated with his class at Yale. After the war he lived on family farm and served in the Connecticut General Assembly. In 1797 he was instrumental in seeking a separate township for North Stratford to be known as Trumbull, Connecticut. His son Gideon served as governor of Connecticut from 1827 to 1831.

He died on January 14, 1849, at the age of eighty-nine. In this daguerreotype, probably taken not long before his death, he grips his cane in his right hand and gazes intently into the camera, while his other hand rests on the arm of the chair. His heavy overcoat suggests that it was taken in the winter.

…mer Tyler (March 1, 1775–July 7, 1866)

…cal Society

… the request of her children and grandchil-
…s and literary Mary Tyler wrote a mem-
… her birth to the War of 1812. Known as
…'s *Book,* it remained in family hands to be
… aloud to each new generation of Tyler children, until it was given to the Vermont Historical Society in 1936.

Using notes compiled by her mother, Elizabeth Hunt Palmer, and her own childhood memories, she combined her mother's remembrances of the Boston Tea Party and of rescuing her baby (Mary) from the Battle of Lexington with her own experiences of seeing French officers visiting her grandfather and being present at the inauguration of George Washington.

Tyler's everyday life and family history were intertwined with the American Revolution. Both her father, Joseph P. Palmer, and her grandfather, Joseph Palmer, served as generals in the war, her grandfather as a brigadier general. Only eight years old at the conclusion of the conflict, she always remembered the end of the war. "About this time, I recollect, we children were playing on the floor in the parlor. I was lying down on the carpet when my father rushed into the house, threw open the door of the room saying, 'Hurrah, Hurrah!' And catching me up in his arms, danced a hornpipe round the room singing and whistling in a very extraordinary manner" (*Grandmother Tyler's Book*).

In 1794 she secretly married Royall Tyler, a veteran and a literary figure, against her parents' wishes. They kept their clandestine union private for two years. At the time of their marriage, he was already well known for writing *The Contrast* (1787), a comedy written for the stage. He was eighteen years her senior.

While in her thirties, she wrote *The Maternal Physician: A Treatise in the Nature and Management of Infants* (1818), a nineteenth-century guide to childhood illnesses. She dedicated it to her mother for "the sublime lesson that the best pleasures of a woman's life are found in the faithful discharge of her maternal duties."

At the end of her recollections about the beginnings of this country, she concluded, "If I should attempt to record all the incidents and events of the last fifty years of my life, my strength and your patience would be exhausted; there I bid you adieu. I am now eighty-eight years and eight months old" (*Grandmother Tyler's Book*). She began writing in May 1858 and didn't finish until November 1863, five and half years later.

In this daguerreotype of Mary in a day cap, she gazes at the photographer with intelligent eyes, a kindly look, and a slight smile upon her wrinkled face, while her dark hair belies her age. Mary Tyler died on July 7, 1866, in her ninety-second year, having lived through yet another war.

Nicholas G. Veeder (December 25, 1761–December 7, 1862)
From the Collection of the Schenectady County Historical Society

Born on Christmas Day to Gerrit Veeder and Anneke DeGraf, Veeder died three weeks short of his one hundredth birthday. In his original pension application, Veeder recalled that he served several tours of duty, some for only a few days at a time. His various assignments included escorting prisoners to Ballston prison, garrison duty at Fort Paris (Stone Arabia), New York, and routing Tories. He also became a scout with a band of Oneida Indians, seeking the arrest of Joseph Bettis, a well-known British spy.

In 1855, at the age of ninety-three, Veeder applied for a bounty land grant and recalled his service differently, stating that he enrolled in 1777 at sixteen as a private in Capt. Jesse Van Slyck's Regiment of New York militia commanded by Col. Abraham Wemple. He lacked documentation for his service and testified that "all witnesses to his services are deceased."

It wasn't his military service that led to his legendary reputation but his fascination with Revolutionary War memorabilia. After the war, Nicholas Veeder returned home to Schenectady County, New York, became a boat builder of some note, and opened a museum of war relics known as the Old Fort in his home on Scotia's Halcyon Street. His collection was a popular destination for tourists seeking a glimpse of the oldest living local survivor of the Revolution. He offered visitors tours of local landmarks, entertaining them along the way with his war stories. Here he's posed in front of his museum in full military regalia—complete with a tricorn hat—surrounded by muskets and a Liberty flag.

Nathan Walden Jr. (January 14, 1762–May 23, 1855)
Collection of Crane Walden

Very little is known about this portrait of Walden. A descendant owns a copy of the daguerreotype, but the location of the original is unknown. His steely resolve is apparent in the way he looks directly into the camera and firmly grips a cane in one hand and a book in the other.

During the Revolutionary War, Walden enlisted at Westfield, Massachusetts, and served as a private under Colonel Holbrook in the 4th Massachusetts Regiment. In 1778, a cannon ball hit him in the head at the Battle of Quaker Hill, Rhode Island, causing permanent deafness and problems with his eyesight. He was taken prisoner at the Battle of White Plains, New York, and spent almost a year in captivity in New York City. Despite his infirmities, Walden continued his military service until 1781. He received a pension in 1818 but was dropped from the rolls in 1820. Men who had means of support did not qualify in 1820. He was reinstated in 1833.

In 1849, Walden wrote to the pension department, describing his circumstances and the accident: "When Congress passed the act of 1818, granting compensation to the Revolutionary Soldiers, In my report to the War Office & my name was entered on the pension role, at the rate of eight dollars per month. I received the pay for the year & a half as right as I can remember." He continued, saying that in 1820 Congress passed the act for the benefit of paupers, and at that point he was able to take care of himself: "But it is different with me now I am old and feeble & unable to provide for myself, having received a shot from the cannon of the enemies at the Battle of Quaker hill, in the expedition for Rhode Island, in 1778 which carried away part of the Crown of my hat, It gave my head such severe shock, as to make me instantly deaf . . . and of my eyes that I can not see to read" (Pension Records). It was an impassioned plea for additional financial assistance.

Daniel Waldo (September 10, 1762–July 30, 1864)
Collection of David Allen Lambert

Hillard referred to Waldo as "the most widely known of the surviving soldiers of the Revolution." While Hillard arrived at Waldo's house after his decease, he included a biography and photograph of him in his *Last Men of the Revolution.*

Born in Windham, Connecticut, Waldo was drafted as a soldier at the age of sixteen for one month of service in the Connecticut militia and later enlisted for an additional term. According to his pension application, he was taken prisoner in December 1779 and released in February 1780 from the infamous Sugar House Prison in New York, which was known for its cruel treatment of inmates. In his 1833 pension application, he told about the events of his capture: "Whilst on the 25th day of December a.s. 1779, I was stationed as a sentinel at the door of the house of Colonel Wells. I together with twenty or more including the Colonel were taken prisoners by the refuges [*sic*] or cow boys." He is known as the last living Revolutionary War prisoner.

After the war he graduated from Yale, became a Congregational minister, married, and had children. According to his obituary in the *(Baltimore) Sun,* he was elected chaplain of the House of Representatives in 1856. On July 19, 1856, the first session of the 34th Congress increased his pension following his service.

Many of the photographs of him show him standing as if at a pulpit. Here he stands with his hand resting on the balustrade and column in the photographer's studio as if ready to give a sermon.

His death was preceded by a fall down a flight of stairs at his home in Syracuse. At the time of his demise, the *Philadelphia Inquirer* called him "Father Waldo," reporting that even at 102 years of age he was healthy and strong and citing that he had recently preached two sermons in one Sunday.

There are several different cartes de visite of Waldo from the 1860s, including this one taken by photographers Churchill and Denison of New York.

Abraham Wheelwright (July 26, 1757–October 14, 1850)
History of the Marine Society of Newburyport, Massachusetts

At eighty years old, Wheelwright wrote a personal reminiscence of his Revolutionary War exploits, naming each of the ships on which he served as an ensign. It appeared as a "Narrative of the adventures of a sailor and soldier in the American Revolution from January, 1776 to February 1777" (in Bailey and Jones, *History of the Marine Society of Newburyport, Massachusetts . . .*). It's a remarkable account of one man's wartime experiences.

In his pension application he told of learning of the Battle of Lexington and Concord while on board a ship off the coast of Newfoundland. His only nonmarine service was the thirteen and a half months he served as a soldier in 1776, joining at Winter Hill, Massachusetts, in Capt. Enoch Putnam's Company, Cdr. Israel Hutchinson's Regiment. He recalled his company's move to fortify Dorchester before moving on to New London. He was part of the regiment that escaped in the heavy fog after the Battle of New London. In both New London and New York his company worked on fortifications. Despite their efforts, the British took New York in August 1776. In December his company crossed the Delaware with Washington's troops, capturing the Hessians at Trenton, New Jersey, on December 26, 1776. In his pension application of 1832, Wheelwright said he was also at the Battle of Princeton. He remained in the army at their winter quarters in Morristown while the British were at Brunswick, New Jersey. Wheelwright was discharged in February 1777.

Two years later he enlisted on an armed schooner under the command of John Holms. He sailed to Guadeloupe, engaging in skirmishes en route. He recounted what happened after they encountered a British ship: "I received a stroke on my head with a cutlass, the scar now visible, from the first stroke, with the cry [']who are you?[']" The prisoners were put on a ship home, but winds took them to Ireland. "Here I concocted a plan to get away from our captors" (Bailey and Jones, *History of the Marine Society of Newburyport, Massachusetts . . .*, 346). Wheelwright made a deal with the captain, who supposedly found the men passage home on a ship bound for the West Indies. For several days they were successful in escaping the press gangs roaming the wharves, intent on impressing sailors to man ships. Wheelwright was offered a berth on a ship but didn't want to accept because it was armed and could involve him in fighting his countrymen. Instead, the captain reportedly said, "[']You are an honest fellow[,'] and no further attempt was made to persuade or force a complyance." Each man was assigned a position and paid for their work. Wheelwright finally returned home in 1780, got married, and signed on as mate on another ship. According to details supplied in his pension papers, on his last voyage he was taken prisoner and sent to Bermuda. While this account doesn't agree with his memoir, it is certain he was taken prisoner at some point during the war, but only he knew if the discrepancies were due to faulty memory or embellishment of his account of events.

John Williams
103 years old

John Williams (c. 1766–October 14, 1870)
Collection of Theresa Franks

Only fragments of John Williams's life remain to tell his story—a brief obituary and a few census records. The rest of his tale is lost history. Yet from these small details it's possible to piece together some of his life.

"In this city, on the 14th inst., Mr. John Williams, (colored) aged nearly 108 years. Funeral from the Clayton Street Church, on Sunday afternoon, at 2 o'clock. Relatives and friends are invitedt [*sic*] to attend," read his death notice in the October 16, 1874, *Providence Journal.* His official death record listed the cause of death as old age and his occupation as a mason.

Rhode Island was a key port in the triangle trade of rum, sugar, and slaves that kept the colonial economy vigorous. Efforts by Quakers, Baptists, and Congregationalists toward emancipation steadily reduced the number of slaves in the colony from more than four thousand in 1755 to slightly more than three thousand in 1774. If Williams's age was correct in the obituary, his year of birth was 1766 or 1767, and he probably spent his childhood as a slave. Throughout the Revolutionary War, these Rhode Islanders fought for another type of liberty—freedom from slavery. In 1784, the Rhode Island General Assembly voted for gradual emancipation that specified that children born as of March 1, 1784, to slaves were free but would continue to live as slaves until they were twenty-one, but those born before that date were slaves for life. According to Sydney James in *Colonial Rhode Island,* the Quaker community sought to make newly freed slaves self-sufficient through education. The last slave born in Rhode Island died in that state in 1859.

In the 1850 and 1860 federal censuses, Williams told the enumerators he was born in Rhode Island, but in the subsequent schedule for 1870 he reported his birthplace as Africa. It's difficult to know if Williams was actually brought into the colony as a child by a Rhode Island slaver or if his story became embellished with time. It is likely that his surname came from the family who owned him, but his actual parentage is unknown. It's also possible that he was born to free blacks. In the late eighteenth century, there was a large population of free blacks in Providence, as opposed to Newport's large slave community.

Williams appears in the 1850 Census as a laborer living alone at age seventy-five, and in 1860 as a jobber aged ninety. In 1870, at the age of 102, he was living with seventy-year-old Sarah J. Williams. His notoriety as a centenarian was growing, because he had posed for two photographs. Photographer Stephen A. Dexter took this carte de visite of him at 103 with cane in hand and a photographer's brace holding him still for the camera, and his competitors, the Manchester Brothers' studio, posed Williams seated at a small table with his cane and a top hat at his feet. It's unknown if these images were taken for family, or if both photographers approached him because of his reputation as one of Rhode Island's last vestiges of the infamous slave trade.

Huldah Welles Wolcott (1760–February 3, 1860)
Connecticut Historical Society, Hartford, Connecticut

In 1790, Huldah Welles, daughter of Ichabod and Abigail Welles, married widower and Revolutionary War veteran William Wolcott. During the war, Wolcott served three different terms—six months in 1776 and two months in 1777, both with Capt. Chester Welles, as part of the Connecticut state troops. He enlisted for another month in 1780.

Wolcott stated in his 1832 pension application that in 1776 he was in New York when the British landed on Long Island and that he was present in Trenton on Christmas Day. His duties in New York were to guard Tories. He was in Danbury, Connecticut, in April 1777 soon after the British under Governor Tryon burned the stores. He had no proof of his birth in 1754; he affirmed that his "birth [was] recorded by his father in the family bible" (Pension Records). William died March 11, 1841.

This common man from Wethersfield saw no battlefield service but listed all the famous generals he saw while "on the town in New York"—Washington, Sullivan (taken on Long Island), Green(e), Parson, Putnam, and Lee, and he thought he had spotted General Arnold but stated he wasn't sure. He no longer knew anyone in his regiment and remarked "that he was not drafted but enlisted voluntarily."

Huldah Wolcott applied for her widow's rights in 1848, seven years after William's death in 1841. She continued to receive his $33.33 annual pension. Upon her death at ninety-nine years six months ten days on February 3, 1860, she was the oldest person in Wethersfield.

At some point, perhaps for her ninetieth birthday in 1850, Huldah Wolcott visited the daguerreotype studio of African American and Connecticut photographer Augustus Washington. For the portrait she wore her "best black silk" dress from 1837–38. Her huge gigot sleeves date the dress. Huldah's slight smile is charming as she stiffly holds a book, maybe a Bible, her face framed by her ruffled cap.

Joseph Wood Jr. (November 8, 1759–December 17, 1859)
Collection of Sandra MacLean Clunies

Joseph Wood Jr.'s father recruited his sons for the militia in the patriotic town of Lebanon, New Hampshire. Joseph Wood Sr., along with every adult male in the community, signed the Association Test in support of the American Revolution. His son Joseph served active duty in 1777 before turning eighteen. His age and inexperience were not unusual during this war.

During the Revolution he served first at Ticonderoga and Stillwater in Captain Hendee's Company and Colonel Chase's Regiment for three months. It wasn't until 1781 that he rejoined with Captain Nelson's Company, Colonel Waite's Regiment, for six months at Corinth. A subsequent enlistment in 1782 brought him home after the burning of Royalton, Vermont. He also served after the war as a captain of the New Hampshire militia in the War of 1812. In 1832 he received a pension for fifteen months of total service during the Revolution and applied for bounty land in 1855, even though he was already a wealthy man.

Wood was a bit of character. Although an educated man, he never attended Dartmouth College but always made it to their annual commencement beginning in 1771. In 1857, at the age of ninety-seven, a reporter for the *Farmer's Cabinet* remarked that Wood "partook of Gov. Wentworth's barbecued ox, and now vividly describes the festivities of that inauguration of Commencements. He is still vigorous in mind and body, doing a smart day's work in his garden." Wood gave one thousand dollars to help establish the Tilden Ladies Seminary where later generations of Wood women were schooled.

According to genealogist and descendant Sandra MacLean Clunies, Wood was photographed on his one hundredth birthday. The town hosted a great celebration for this significant birthday in November 1859 for Wood, as their first centenarian. One month later they honored him at his funeral. In his will, Clunies reports that "he bequeathed today's value of $150,000 to his huge family, but that he bribed them—promised a colt to every grandson named for himself and a string of gold beads to every granddaughter named for wife Sarah (Gerrish) Wood. . . . So, of course, each of his children had a Joseph and a Sarah!" (e-mail).

Sarah "Sally" Sayward Barrell Keating Wood (1759–1855)
Maine Women Writers Collection, Westbrook College, Portland, Maine

This remarkable woman was Maine's first novelist. Born while her father, Lt. Nathaniel Barrell, was away fighting with Wolfe in Quebec in the French and Indian War, she spent her childhood living with her grandfather, Judge Jonathan Sayward, a Loyalist, in York. Sayward was a merchant, a financial investor, and a member of the Massachusetts General Court. Through her grandfather, Wood met notable Revolutionary War figures such as John Hancock and his wife, John Adams, and members of the Sewall family.

Sayward had participated in the Battle at Louisbourg during the French and Indian War and brought home bounty from the battle. As a merchant and an outspoken Loyalist, he didn't support the Boston Tea Party or the War for Independence. Because of his views, townspeople asked him to account for his politics, but they didn't take any action against him. After the war, Sayward was gradually reaccepted into the York community despite his declaration of his lack of support for the war into the 1780s.

Wood married her first husband, Loyalist Richard Keating, a clerk in her grandfather's business, on November 23, 1778. She bore him three children, the last after his death in 1783.

It was during her twenty-one years as a widow that she began to write novels using the pen name "A Lady from Massachusetts." Between 1800 and 1804 she published four novels.

In 1804, she married Revolutionary War veteran Gen. Abiel Wood and lived in Wiscasset, Maine. After his death in 1811 she wrote just one more book. In her second widowhood, she was well known as much for her writing as for her clothing. She wore high turbans and positioned her bonnets so that they obscured her face. In this daguerreotype her unusual style of headwear is apparent. Her ruffled day cap is antiquated for the 1850s, being of similar design to the directoire bonnet, first introduced in the late 1790s, with its high crown.

Toward the end of her life she wrote sketches of her life for family and friends but never published again.

Also consulted: American War of Independence, 1775–83, www.americanrevolution.org; "Annual Report of the Secretary of the Interior," *Farmer's Cabinet (New Hampshire),* December 30, 1852, 2; "The Annual Reports," *Pittsfield (Massachusetts) Sun,* December 11, 1856, 2; J. Hunter Barbour, "Shadows of Men Who Marched with Washington," *Colonial Williamsburg* 27, no. 2 (2005): 27–31; Joseph Bauman, "Older Americans: A Selection of Primary Citizens," *Daguerreian Society Newsletter* 9, no. 1 (1997): 13–19; "Curious Statistics among Pensioners," *Philadelphia Inquirer,* April 29, 1894, 5; George C. Gilmore, *The First Fourteen Survivors of the Revolutionary Army* (Concord: n.p., 1898); "The Heroes of the Revolution: Personal Sketches of the War of Independence," *New York Herald,* December 31, 1859, 2; "The Last Half Dozen: Portraits of Six Veterans of the Revolution," *Topeka Weekly Capital,* February 26, 1891, 11; "Nearly a Million Paid by Uncle Sam," *Philadelphia Inquirer,* October 19, 1903, 15; "New Publications," *Daily Evening Transcript,* December 24, 1852, 1; "[New York; Revolutionary; March]," *Easton Gazette,* April 9, 1859, 1; "The Old Soldier by H. Hastings Weid," *New Albany Daily Ledger,* December 16, 1854, 1; "The Pension System," *Farmer's Cabinet (New Hampshire),* January 5, 1859, 2; Harold Francis Pfister, *Facing the Light: Historic American Portrait Daguerreotypes; An Exhibition . . .* (Washington, D.C.: Smithsonian Institution Press, 1978); "The Roll of Honor," *(Washington, D.C.) Constitution,* August 31, 1859, 2; "Surviving Women of the Revolution," *New York Herald,* December 31, 1859, 3; "U.S. Pensioners," *Pittsfield Sun,* May 25, 1854, 1; Benson J. Lossing, *Pictorial Field-Book of the Revolution* (New York: Harper and Brothers, 1852), CD Heritage Books, 2004; Benjamin S. Beck, "The Impact of Photography on Quaker Attitudes to Portraiture," *Genealogists Magazine,* June 2001, 21–24; Maureen Taylor, *Uncovering Your Ancestry through Family Photographs,* 2nd ed. (Cincinnati: Family Tree Books, 2005).

SOURCES

Portraits

Note on arrangement: Sources appear in the order of use in the vignettes. Square brackets denote a name not physically found on the image.

Molly Ferris Akin

[Molly Ferris Akin], daguerreotype in the collection of Tyler Burns; e-mail from Tyler Burns to David Allen Lambert, June 16, 2006; Walter Dotts, address to Akin Hall Association, August 14, 1994; Church of Jesus Christ of Latter-day Saints [LDS], "IGI," database, Molly Ferris family group record, www.familysearch.org (accessed Jan. 19, 2007). Also consulted: James H. Smith, *History of Duchess [sic] County, New York: With illustrations and biographical sketches of some of its prominent men and pioneers* (Syracuse, N.Y.: D. Mason and Co., 1882); 1850 U.S. Census, Dutchess County, New York, population schedule, p. 235, dwelling 754, family 254, Mulaby Akin, digital image, www.ancestry.com, citing National Archives, microfilm M432; Gertrude A. Barber, comp., *Deaths Taken from the "Brooklyn Eagle,"* vols. 1–27 (n.p., 1963–66).

James Allen Jr.

"James Allen Jr.," photographic print, Maine Memory Network, www.mainememory.net, image no. 14670; James Allen, Revolutionary War Pension Files, file no. R12085, www.footnote.com; William Wallace Harris and Charles Allyn, *The Battle of Groton Heights: A Collection of Narratives, Official Reports, Records, Etc. of the Storming of Fort Griswold* (New London, Conn.: Charles Allyn, 1882). Also consulted: 1820 U.S. Census, Oxford County, Maine, Turner, p. 127 (upper left corner), p. 224 (penned upper left), line 8, James Allen, digital image, ProQuest, Heritage Quest Online, citing National Archives, microfilm M33, roll 37; 1830 U.S. Census, Oxford County, Maine, Canton, p. 186 (penned upper left), line 3, James Allen, digital image, www.ancestry.com, citing National Archives, microfilm M19, roll 50; 1840 U.S. census, Oxford County, Maine, Canton, p. 222 (stamped), line 13, James Allen, digital image, www.ancestry.com, citing National Archives, microfilm M704, roll 147; 1850 U.S. Census, Oxford County, Maine, population schedule, Canton, p. 121 (stamped), p. 241 (penned upper right), dwelling 9, family 9, James Allen, digital image, www.ancestry.com, citing National Archives, microfilm M432, roll 263; 1860 U.S. Census, Oxford County, Maine, population schedule, Canton, p. 545 (penned upper right), dwelling 150, family 174, James Allen, digital image, ProQuest, Heritage Quest Online, citing National Archives, microfilm M653, roll 444; e-mail from Fran Pollitt to Maureen Taylor, November 7, 2007.

Nathaniel Ames

Samuel Marsden Brookes, Nathaniel Ames, oil, c. 1859, located at the Wisconsin Historical Museum, accession number 1942.199; "Nathaniel Ames, the Revolutionary Patriot," *Wisconsin Daily Patriot,* September 3, 1863, 1; Church of Jesus Christ of Latter-day Saints [LDS], "Ancestral File," database, Irene Waldo family group record, submitted by Wade C. Starks, VeValee (Mann) Reid, and Laurence A. Briggs, www.familysearch.org (accessed Jan. 19, 2007); Revolutionary War Pension Files, Nathaniel Ames, file no. S11979/BLWT5215-160-55, www.footnote.com; "Burial of Nathaniel Ames, the Last of the Revolutionary Fathers," *Wisconsin Patriot,* September 3, 1863, 7. Also consulted: "A Connecticut Revolutionary Patriot," *Historical Magazine,* October 1863, 318; "Nathaniel Ames," in *American Historical Record,* ed. Benson J. Lossing (Philadelphia: Samuel P. Town, 1873), 534; "Nathaniel Ames, the Soldier of the Revolution," *Wisconsin Patriot,* May 9, 1863, 7; Charles Nelson, "Our Namesake: Nathaniel Ames, Patriot," Wisconsin Society, Sons of the American Revolution, www.wissar.org/ames.htm (accessed Oct. 20, 2007); "Report on the Picture Gallery," *Collections of the State Historical Society of Wisconsin* 4 (1857–58): 110.

George Avery
Jane G. (Avery) Carter and Susie P. Holmes, *Genealogical Record of the Dedham Branch of the Avery Family in America* (Plymouth, Mass.: Press of Avery and Doten, 1893); Revolutionary War Pension Files, George Avery, file no. W23477/BLWT26129–160–55, www.footnote.com; Ivah Dunklee, *Burning of Royalton, Vermont by Indians: A careful research of all that pertains to the subject, including a reprint of Zadock Steele's narrative, also a complete account of the various anniversaries and the placing of a monument commemorating the event, has herein been made* (Boston: G. H. Ellis Co., 1906); *U.S. Pensioners, 1818–1872* [database online, www.ancestry.com], Provo, Utah, Generations Network, 2007, original data from Ledgers of Payments, 1818–72, to U.S. Pensioners under Acts of 1818 through 1858 from Records of the Office of the Third Auditor of the Treasury, 1818–72, National Archives, microfilm T718, 23 rolls, Records of the Accounting Officers of the Department of the Treasury, RG 217, National Archives, Washington, D.C. (accessed Oct. 15, 2009).

Anna Warner Bailey
"Anna Bailey," photographic print, n.d., located at Monument House Museum at Fort Griswold, Groton, Connecticut; Carol Kimball, "Our Petticoat Heroine," Anna Warner Bailey Chapter National Society of the Daughters of the American Revolution, www.rootsweb.ancestry.com/~ctawbcd/awbailey.htm (accessed Jan. 24, 2007); "Mother Bailey," *(Connecticut) Morning News,* January 18, 1847, 2; "Mother Bailey," *(Connecticut) Constitution,* February 10, 1847, 1; Mary Simmerson Cunningham Logan, *The Part Taken by Women in American History* (Wilmington, Del.: Perry-Nalle, 1912); Benson J. Lossing, *Pictorial Field-Book of the Revolution* (New York: Harper and Brothers, 1860), CD Heritage Books, 2004, 1:617–18; "Anna Bailey," www.americanrevolution.org; "Mother Bailey," *Boston Daily Evening Transcript,* October 19, 1849, 2; "One Hundred and Fifteenth Anniversary of the Battle of Fort Griswold," Historical paper given before the Minneapolis Chapter, Daughters of the American Revolution . . . by Mrs. Jennie J. B. Goodwin in Daughters of the American Revolution, ed. Mrs. Mary S. Lockwood, *American Monthly Magazine* 9 (July–December 1896): 428–33; Frances Lester Roland, "Mother Bailey," in historical paper given before the Minneapolis Chapter, Daughters of the American Revolution, edited by Mrs. Mary S. Lockwood, *American Monthly Magazine* 9 (July–December 1896): 433–36.

Daniel Frederick Bakeman
Reverend E. B. Hillard, *The Last Men of the Revolution* (1864; repr., Barre, Mass.: Barre, 1968); Bills and Resolutions, House of Representatives, 39th Congress, 2nd sess., read twice and referred to the Committee on Pensions, "An Act for the Relief of Daniel Frederick Bakeman, a Revolutionary Soldier, January 25, 1867"; Obituary, *Memphis Daily Avalanche,* Apr. 20, 1869, 1; Revolutionary War Pension Files, Daniel Frederick Bakeman, file no. S17665, www.footnote.com; A. D. Cross, original carte de visite of Daniel Frederick Bakeman, Massachusetts, 1868; "Fought in the Revolution: Sketch of Life of Last Survivor of War for Independence," *Duluth News Tribune,* May 31, 1903, 4. Also consulted: James F. Morrison, "Morrison's Pensions: Who Was the Last Surviving Soldier of the Revolution?" *Morrison's Pensions,* http://morrisonspensions.org/bakeman.html, 2007 (accessed Oct. 20, 2007); Donald H. Piron Jr., "The Last Surviving Soldier of the American Revolution . . . My Fourth Great Grandfather," *Empire Patriot,* February 2003; Carl F. Bessent, "Revolutionary Longevity," *SAR Magazine* 73 (Spring 1979): 4.

Amos Baker
Unknown artist, "Amos Baker," hand-colored photographic print, in the collection of the Concord [Massachusetts] Free Library; "The Concord Fight: Affidavit to the Last Survivor," *Connecticut Courant,* May 18, 1850, 78; "The Contoy Prisoners," *Vermont*

Journal, August 2, 1850, 1; Revolutionary War Pension Files, Amos Baker, file no. S4922, www.footnote.com; "Celebration at Concord," *Boston Daily Evening Transcript*, April 20, 1850, 1; *Letter to Lemuel Shattuck, ESQ. of Boston from Josiah Adams, ESQ. of Framingham in Vindication of the Claims of Capt. Isaac Davis, of Acton* (Boston: Damrell and Moore, 1850); "Mysterious Militia Man Deserts at Old North Bridge," *Concord Magazine*, www.concordma.com/magazine/marapr01/mysterman.html (accessed Feb. 28, 2007).

Mary (Seeley) Batterson

[Mary Batterson], ambrotype, in the collection of David Batterson Hughes; William Richard Cutter, *Genealogical and Family History of the State of Connecticut* (New York: Lewis Historical Publishing, 1911); Revolutionary War Pension Files, Widow's Pension, file no. W17257/BLWT2356-160-55, www.footnote.com. Also consulted: 1850 U.S. Census, Litchfield County, Connecticut, population schedule, Warren, p. 89 (stamped), p. 207 (penned upper right), dwelling 1321, family 1396, Frederick R. Smith, digital image, www.ancestry.com, citing National Archives, microfilm M432, roll 43; pedigree chart submitted by Dave and Marilyn Hughes, n.d.

Hannah (Paxson) and Jesse Betts

Benjamin Betts, daguerreotypist, [Hannah Betts], n.d., private collection; unknown daguerreotypist, [Jesse Betts], n.d., private collection; e-mail from Jeanne Powell to Maureen Taylor, June 18, 2007; Karin A. Wulf, *"Despite the mean distinctions [these] Times Have made": The Complexity of Patriotism and Quaker Loyalism in One Pennsylvania Family*, www.revolution.h-net.msu.edu/essays/wulf.html (accessed Nov. 13, 2007); 1850 U.S. Census, New Castle County, Delaware, population schedule, Wilmington, p. 113 (stamped), p. 225 (penned upper right), dwelling 1644, family 1699, Jesse Betts, digital image, www.ancestry.com, citing National Archives, microfilm M432, roll 53; "Betts and Steel Records, 1828–1868," finding aid, Hagley Museum and Library, www.hagley.lib.de.us/2179; Church of Jesus Christ of Latter-day Saints [LDS], "Ancestral File," database, Jesse Betts family group record, submitted by Earl Jay Nielson and Charles E. Heinze, www.familysearch.org (accessed Jan. 19, 2007).

Josiah Brown

"Josiah Brown," daguerreotype, in the collections of the Bennington Museum, accession number 2004.28; "Descendants of Thomas Browne," Rootsweb World Connect Project, www.rootsweb.ancestry.com (accessed Nov. 13, 2007); Card file at Bennington Museum for Josiah Brown; Leonard Brown, *History of Whitingham: From Its Organization to the Present Time* (Brattleboro, Vt.: F. E. Housh, 1886); Abby Maria Hemenway, *Vermont: A Historical Gazetteer*, vol. 5, Windham County (Brandon, Vt.: Carrie E. H. Page, 1891), digital file, www.rootsweb.com/~vtwindha/vhg5/vt_gazetteer-whitingham.htm (accessed Nov. 13, 2007).

Caesar

"Caesar: A slave," daguerreotype, c. 1850, cased photograph file, PR-012-002-323, located at the New-York Historical Society; William Byrk, "Remembering New York's Bleak History," *New York Sun*, October 7, 2005, Arts and Letters, www.americanhistoryworkshop.com/news/nysun051007.htm (accessed Feb. 28, 2007); Simon Schama, *Rough Crossings: Britain, the Slaves, and the American Revolution* (New York: HarperCollins, 2006); Florence A. Christoph and Peter R. Christoph, *Records of the People of the Town of Bethlehem, Albany County, New York, 1698–1880* (Selkirk, N.Y.: Bethlehem Historical Association, 1982); Matthew Nugent, "Nugent/Consolloy Genealogy," Rootsweb World Connect Project, www.worldconnect.rootsweb.com/cgi-bin/igm.cgi (accessed Nov. 14, 2007); Douglas Harper, "Slavery in New York," 2003, www.slavenorth.com/newyork.htm (accessed Nov. 14, 2007); "New York Slave Law Summary and Record,"

Slavery in America, www.slaveryinamerica.org/geography/slave_laws_NY.htm; "Slavery in New York," exhibit at the New-York Historical Society, October 7, 2005, to March 26, 2006, exhibit also available online, www.slaveryinnewyork.org; Ira Berlin and Leslie Maria Harris, *Slavery in New York* (New York: W. W. Norton, 2005); Cliff Lamere, "Nicoll-Sill Cemetery," www.genealogy.cliffamere.com/Aid/Cem/CEM-NicollSill.htm (accessed Nov. 14, 2007). Also consulted: Sidney Kaplan, *The Black Presence in the Era of the American Revolution, 1770–1800* (Washington, D.C.: National Portrait Gallery and the Smithsonian Institution, 1973); Cynthia Kirk, *Coming Face-to-Face with the History of Slavery in New York City,* Feb. 19, 2006, www.voanews.com/specialenglish/archive/2006-02/2006-02-19-voa2.cfm (accessed Nov. 14, 2007).

Noah Callender

[Noah Callender], daguerreotype, n.d., in the collection of the Vermont Historical Society; L. E. Chittenden, *The Capture of Ticonderoga: Annual Address before the Vermont Historical Society* (Ticonderoga, N.Y.: Vermont Historical Society, 1872); Ethan Allen, *A Narrative of Colonel Ethan Allen's Captivity* (1779; repr., n.p.: Thomas and Thomas, 1807); Church of Jesus Christ of Latter-day Saints [LDS], "International Genealogical Index," database, www.familysearch.org, family group record, "Noah Callender Mortuary Notice," *Boston Daily Evening Transcript,* September 2, 1851, 2. Also consulted: 1800 U.S. Census, Addison County, Vermont, Shoreham, ProQuest, Heritage Quest Online, entry for Noah Callender, Shoreham, Addison County, Vermont, 1800; 1830 U.S. Census, Addison County, Vermont, Shoreham, Heritage Quest Online, entry for Noah Callender, Shoreham, Addison County, Vermont, 1830; 1840 U.S. Census, Addison County, Vermont, ProQuest, Heritage Quest Online, entry for Noah Callender, Shoreham, Addison County, Vermont, 1840.

Ezra Carpenter

[Ezra Carpenter], photographic print, n.d., in the collection of Laura Prescott; Amos B. Carpenter, *A Genealogical History of the Rehoboth Branch of the Carpenter Family in America* (Amherst, Mass.: Carpenter and Moore House, 1898); Revolutionary War Pension Files, Ezra Carpenter, file no. W15628, www.footnote.com; e-mails from Laura Prescott to Maureen Taylor, June 6, 7, 11, and July 1, 2007; letter prepared by Harold Milton Prescott, San Francisco, California, November 1916.

Chainbreaker

Jeanne Winston Adler, ed., *Chainbreaker's War* (New York: Black Dome Press. 2002); Frederick Webb Hodge, *Handbook of American Indians North of Mexico* (Washington, D.C.: GPO, 1912); Thomas Donaldson, *Extra Census Bulletin: Indians; The Six Nations of New York* (Washington, D.C.: U.S. Census Printing Office, 1892). Also consulted: Thomas S. Abler, "Governor Blacksnake as a Young Man? Speculation on the Identity of Trumbull's the Young Sachem," *Ethnohistory* 34, no. 4 (1987): 329–51; Blacksnake, Tah-won-ne-ahs, Wolf Clan (c. 1749–1859), Rochester Museum and Science Center, www.rmsc.org/museum/exhibits/online/lhm/blacksnake.htm (accessed Jan. 26, 2007).

Lemuel Cook

Reverend E. B. Hillard, *The Last Men of the Revolution* (1864; repr., Barre, Mass.: Barre, 1968); [Death notice], *Daily Constitutional Union,* May 23, 1866, 1; "Death of a Revolutionary Soldier," *Iowa State Daily Register,* May 31, 1866, 2; Mortuary notice, *Pittsfield Sun,* May 24, 1866, 2; Revolutionary War Pension File, Lemuel Cook, file no. S33258/BLWT5670-100-1790/BLWT86-60-55, www.footnote.com. Also consulted: "The Last Revolutionary Pensioner in New England, and the Last but one upon the Rolls," paper read before the Maine Historical Society on the 19th of

February 1874 by Hon. Joseph Williamson, *American Historical Record,* ed. Benson J. Lossing (Philadelphia: John E. Potter, 1874), 241–44; "Lemuel Cook: Oldest Survivor of the Revolution," Order of the Founders and Patriots of America, www.founderspatriots.org/articles_cook.htm (accessed Feb. 6, 2003).

Samuel Curtis

M. Chandler, [Samuel Curtis], daguerreotype, Marshfield, Massachusetts, 1879, collection of the author; Chris Steele and Ron Polito, *A Directory of Massachusetts Photographers* (Rockland, Maine: Picton Press, 1993); Robert M. Sherman and Ruth Wilder Sherman, *Vital Records of Marshfield, Massachusetts to the Year 1850* (Warwick, R.I.: Society of Mayflower Descendants in the State of Rhode Island, 1970); "A Centenarian's Death," *Boston Daily Advertiser,* August 25, 1879, 2; "Massachusetts Soldiers and Sailors in the War of the Revolution," 17 vols. [database online, www.ancestry.com], Provo, Utah, Generations Network, 2007, original data from Secretary of the Commonwealth, *Massachusetts Soldiers and Sailors in the War of the Revolution,* vols. 1–17 (Boston: Wright and Potter, 1896), 4:271.

George Washington Parke Custis

"George Washington Parke Custis," daguerreotype, 1849, Library of Congress, Dag no. 207; "Mr. Custis at New York," *New-Hampshire Patriot and State Gazette,* August 28, 1845, 4; "History of Arlington to 1861," Custis-Lee Mansion: Robert E. Lee Memorial, December 2, 2002, www.cr.nps.gov/history/online_books/hh/6/hh6b.htm (accessed Jan. 30, 2007); Church of Jesus Christ of Latter-day Saints [LDS], "Ancestral File," database, www.familysearch.org, George Washington Parke Custis family group record (accessed July 23, 2007); Benson J. Lossing, *Pictorial Field-Book of the Revolution* (New York: Harper and Brothers, 1860), CD Heritage Books, 2004; Charles Moore, *The Family Life of George Washington* (Boston: Houghton Mifflin, 1926).

Elizabeth Cutler

"Mrs. Simeon Cutler, Elizabeth Rockwood Cutler, the War of the Revolution, began early in her married life," daguerreotype, c. 1845, Leland Family Papers, Mss 882, R. Stanton Avery Special Collections, New England Historic Genealogical Society; Rev. Abner A. M. Morse, *A Genealogical Register of the Inhabitants and History of the Towns of Sherborn and Holliston* (Sherborn, Mass.: Press of Damrell and Moore, 1856); Nahum S. Cutler, *A Cutler Memorial and Genealogical History: Containing the Names of a Large Portion of the Cutlers in the United States and Canada, and a Record of Many Individual Members of the Family, with an Account also of Other Families Allied to the Cutlers by Marriage* (Greenfield, Mass.: Press of E. A. Hall and Co., 1889); Wilson Waters, *History of Chelmsford, Massachusetts* (Printed for the town by *Courier-Citizen,* 1917); *Massachusetts Soldiers and Sailors in the War of the Revolution* (Boston: Wright and Potter, 1896–1908), 4:326; "Direct tax list of 1798 for Massachusetts and Maine, 1798," handwritten tax list, twenty folio vols. plus two suppl. vols., donated to New England Historic Genealogical Society (NEHGS) by William Henry Montague, 1850, R. Stanton Avery Collections, NEHGS, Boston, Massachusetts, listed in *Massachusetts and Maine 1798 Direct Tax,* online database, NEHGS, www.newenglandancestors.org, 2003 (accessed Nov. 18, 2007); *Index to the Probate Records of Middlesex County, Massachusetts,* online database, www.newenglandancestors.org, NEHGS, 2003, originally published by City of Cambridge, Mass., as *Index to the Probate Records of the County of Middlesex, Massachusetts, 1912–14,* Middlesex County, Massachusetts Probate no. 5563 (Simeon Cutler, administration, 1799), LDS film no. 0386067, microfilm available at the NEHGS.

Esther Damon

"Esther Damon," in Merritt L. Dawkins, "Sands of Time," *DAR Magazine* 61, no. 5 (1927): 355; "Last Widow of Revolution," *Bos-*

ton Daily Globe, November 12, 1906, 5; Don Wickman, "The Last Widow," People and Places, *Rutland Daily Herald,* March 7, 2002, C-1, 4; Revolutionary War Pension File, Noah Damon, file no. W10711/BLWT36643–160–55, www.footnote.com.

Simon Dearborn

"Simon Dearborn," daguerreotype, Maine Historical Society; David Dearborn, "Manuscript Genealogy of the Dearborn Family," typescript, August 2004; Revolutionary War Pension Files, Simon Dearborn, file no. S35246, www.footnote.com.

Samuel Downing

Reverend E. B. Hillard, *The Last Men of the Revolution* (1864; repr., Barre, Mass.: Barre, 1968); Revolutionary War Pension File, Samuel Downing, file no. S40,055/BLWT293–60–55/BLWT3067–100, www.footnote.com; "Samuel Downing: The Last Soldier of the Revolution," *Pittsfield Sun,* February 28, 1867. Also consulted: 1800 U.S. Census, Orange County, New York, Newburgh, p. 279 (handwritten), p. 200 (penned upper right), line 16, Samuel Downing, digital image, ProQuest, Heritage Quest Online, citing National Archives, microfilm M32, roll 21; 1810 U.S. Census, Orange County, New York, Newburgh, p. 300 (handwritten along right side), p. 163 (digital index number), line 20, Samuel Downing, digital image, ProQuest, Heritage Quest Online, citing National Archives, microfilm M252, roll 29; 1820 U.S. Census, Orange County, New York, Newburgh, p. 217 (stamped lower right corner), p. 225 (digital number), Samuel Downing, digital image, ProQuest, Heritage Quest Online, citing National Archives, microfilm M33, roll 64; 1830 U.S. Census, Saratoga County, New York, Edinburg, p. 200 (penned upper left), line 24, Samuel Downing, digital image, www.ancestry.com, citing National Archives, microfilm M704, roll 147; 1840 U.S. Census, Saratoga County, New York, Edinburg, p. 200, line 24, Samuel Downing, digital image, www.ancestry.com, citing National Archives, microfilm M704, roll 336; 1850 U.S. Census, Orange County, New York, population schedule, Edinburgh, p. 410 (stamped), p. 817 (stamped), dwelling 178, family 181, Samuel Downing, digital image, www.ancestry.com, citing National Archives, microfilm M432, roll 593.

Pierre Etienne DuPonceau

Robert Cornelius, daguerreotypist, "Pierre Etienne DuPonceau," May 15, 1840, located at the American Philosophical Society, Digid 979; Mark M. Boatner III, *Encyclopedia of the American Revolution* (repr., Mechanicsburg, Penn.: Stackpole Books, 1994), entry for Steuben; John A. Garraty and Mark C. Carnes, *American National Biography* (New York: Oxford Univ. Press, 1999), vol. 7, sv "Du-Ponceau, Pierre Etienne"; "Peter Stephen DuPonceau Collection," American Philosophical Society, www.amphilsoc.org/library/mole/d/duponceau.htm; William F. Stapp, *Robert Cornelius: Portraits from the Dawn of Photography* (Washington, D.C.: Smithsonian Institution Press, 1983); Revolutionary War Pension File, Peter Stephen DuPonceau, file no. S5371/BLWT638, www.footnote.com; Peter S. DuPonceau, *A Brief View of the Constitution of the United States Addressed to the Law Academy of Pennsylvania* (Philadelphia: Law Academy, 1834); "Philadelphia: John Wilcocks, Esq; Nine; Western Insurgents; Marries; Biship Provost; Peter Stephen Duponceau," *(New York) Daily Advertiser,* September 17, 1794, 2; Thomas Willing Balch, "Some Former Members of the American Philosophical Society," *Proceedings of the American Philosophical Society* 51, no. 207 (1912): 580–601; C. R. D. PH. and D. D. Lepsius, *Standard Alphabet for Reducing Unwritten Languages and Foreign Graphic Systems to a Uniform Orthography in European Letters* (London: Williams and Norgate, 1863); "Pierre-Etienne DuPonceau (1760–1844)," finding aid, University of California Library, www.toto.lib.unca.edu/findingaids/mss/speculation_lands/biographies/duponceau.htm; "Discourse on Mr. DuPonceau," *North American and Daily Advertiser,* October 31, 1844, 2.

RALPH FARNHAM

"Ralph Farnham, Aged 102 years, July 7, 1858," ambrotype, July 7, 1858, in the collections of the Massachusetts Historical Society, photo 2.16; O. Henry Mace, *Collector's Guide to Early Photographs* (Iola, Wis.: Krause, 1999); Olive M. Treadwell, *Sesquicentennial History of Acton, Maine, 1830–1980* (n.p., n.d.); Revolutionary War Pension File, Ralph Farnham, file no. S31018/BLWT9451-160-55, www.footnote.com; C. W. Clarence, *A Biographical Sketch of the Life of Ralph Farnham of Acton, Maine* (Boston: n.p., 1860); Megan Friedel, "Ralph Farnham, the Last Survivor of the Battle of Bunker Hill," 2006, www.masshit.org/objects/2005october.cfm (accessed Dec. 1, 2006); "Interview of the Prince with Ralph Farnham," *New York Herald,* October 19, 1860, 4; *The New England Tour of His Royal Highness the Prince of Wales,* 3rd ed. (Boston: Bee Printing, 1860). Also consulted: "Ralph Farnham, the Veteran," *Philadelphia Inquirer,* October 12, 1860, 7; Rev. J. M. W. Farnham, *Genealogy of the Farnham Family* (New York: Baker and Taylor, 1889).

SARAH (STEVENS) FELLOWS

"Sarah Stevens Fellows," photographic print, in the collection of Gayle E. Waite; Revolutionary War Pension Files, Widow's Pension, Moses Fellows, file no. W23030BLWT5375-160-55 www.footnote.com; *Lineage Book of the National Society of Daughters of Founders and Patriots of America,* vol. 25 (Washington, D.C.: Daughters of Founders and Patriots of America, 1937); John J. Dearborn, *History of Salisbury, New Hampshire* (Manchester, N.H.: W. E. Moore, 1890); e-mail from Gayle Waite to Maureen Taylor, November 20, 2007. Also consulted: 1810 U.S. Census, Rockingham County, New Hampshire, Chichester, p. 313 (stamped), p. 159 (pen in upper right), p. 315 (digital index number), line 1, Sarah Fellows, digital image, ProQuest, Heritage Quest Online, citing National Archives, microfilm M252, roll 25.

GEORGE FISHLEY

[George Fishley], daguerreotype, in the collection of Nick Manganiello; J. Dennis Robinson, "The Revolutionary Eyes of George Fishley," As I Please, www.seacostnh.com/arts/please112402.htm (accessed Aug. 5, 2004); "Capt. George Fishley," *Portsmouth (New Hampshire) Journal,* January 4, 1851, 2; Revolutionary War Pension Files, George Fishley, file no. S45764, www.footnote.com; "Deaths," *Portsmouth Journal of Literature and Politics,* May 5, 1839, 3.

ALBERT GALLATIN

Anthony, Edwards and Co., "Albert Gallatin," daguerreotype, copy of a daguerreotype by Mathew Brady [between 1844 and 1860], in the collections of the Library of Congress, Washington, D.C., Dag no. 219; "Decease of the Venerable Albert Gallatin," *Farmer's Cabinet (New Hampshire),* August 23, 1849, 2. Also consulted: Harold Francis Pfister, *Facing the Light: Historic American Portrait Daguerreotypes: An Exhibition* (Washington, D.C.: Smithsonian Institution Press, 1978); "Albert Gallatin (1801–1814)," History of the Treasury: Secretaries of the Treasury," 2001, www.treas.gov/education/history/secretaries/agallatin.shtml (accessed Oct. 27, 2007); Archibald L. Dick, engraver, Howard J. Chilton, photographer, [Albert Gallatin], in *Memoir, prepared at the request of a committee of the Common council of the city of New York . . . 1826,* cataloging record, www.digitalgallery.nypl.org (accessed Jan. 30, 2007); John A. Garraty and Mark C. Carnes, *American National Biography* (New York: Oxford Univ. Press, 1999) vol. 8, sv "Gallatin, Albert"; "Albert Gallatin," *North American and United States Gazette (Pennsylvania),* August 15, 1849, 1.

JOHN GRAY

I. N. Knowlton, "John Gray," photographic print, Ohio, 1868, Library of Congress, Biog. File ; J. M. Dalzell, *John Gray, of Mount Vernon: The Last Soldier of the Revolution* (Washington, D.C.:

Dalzell and Woodburn, 1868); Revolutionary War Pension Files, John Gray, file no. S1464, www.footnote.com; "The Last One Gone," *Idaho Tri-Weekly Statesmen,* May 28, 1868, 2. Also consulted: 1860 U.S. Census, Noble County, Ohio, population schedule, Brookfield Township, p. 424 (stamped), dwelling 362, family 358, John Gray, digital image, ProQuest, Heritage Quest Online, citing National Archives, microfilm M653, roll 1020; Mary Yeates Soule, "John Gray of Mount Vernon: The Last Soldier of the Revolution, Born Near Mount Vernon, Virginia," typescript, 1936.

Dr. Ezra Green

L. T. Brigham, "Dr. Ezra Green," Dover, New Hampshire, in the collection of David Allen Lambert; "Dr. Erza Green; Dover; N.H.; Judge Timothy Narrar; Ipswich; N.H.; John Quincy Adams; Mr. Adams," *Boston Daily Evening Transcript,* June 27, 1844, 4; "Harvard University; Dr. Ezra Green; Dover, N.H.; Malden; Mass; June; New Hampshire," *Farmer's Cabinet (New Hampshire),* September 11, 1845, 2; Clifford K. Shipton, *Biographical Sketches of Those Who Attended Harvard College in the Classes, 1764–1767, Ezra Green* (Boston: Massachusetts Historical Society, 1972); Revolutionary War Rolls, 1775–83, Ezra Green, digital image, www.footnote.com, citing National Archives, microfilm M246, image no. 9691905; Revolutionary War Pension Files, Ezra Green, file no. S430, www.footnote.com; Deloraine Pendre Corey, *The History of Malden Massachusetts, 1633–1785* (Malden: Author, 1899); "Diary of Ezra Green," *New England Historical and Genealogical Register,* online database, www.NewEnglandAncestors.org, New England Historic Genealogical Society, 2001–7 (orig. pub. as New England Historic Genealogical Society, *The New England Historical and Genealogical Register, 1847–2004* (January 1875): 29:13–24; George Henry Preble and Walter C. Green, *Diary of Dr. Ezra Green: Surgeon on Board the Continental Ship-of-War "Ranger" under Capt. John Paul Jones from November 1, 1777, to September 27, 1778* (Boston: Privately printed, 1875); Mortuary notice, *New-Hampshire Sentinel,* July 29, 1847, 3.

Josiah Walpole Hall

"Josiah Hall," photographic print, copy by George S. Raymond, Ogdensburg, N.Y., in the collection of the Godfrey family archives; e-mail from Phillip Burcham to Maureen Taylor, August 2, 2007; Revolutionary War Pension Files, Josiah Hall, file no. S29865/BLWT12820-160-55, www.footnote.com; "Mortuary," *New-Hampshire Sentinel,* July 3, 1855, 3; "Mr. Josiah Hall; Walpole," *Boston Evening Transcript,* January 6, 1855, 1; *U.S. Pensioners, 1818–1872* [database online, www.ancestry.com], Provo, Utah, Generations Network, 2007, original data from Ledgers of Payments, 1818–72, to U.S. Pensioners under Acts of 1818 through 1858 from Records of the Office of the Third Auditor of the Treasury, 1818–72, National Archives, microfilm T718, 23 rolls, Records of the Accounting Officers of the Department of the Treasury, RG 217, National Archives, Washington, D.C. (accessed Oct. 15, 2009).

Jonathan Harrington

[Jonathan Harrington], daguerreotype, in the collections of the Lexington, Massachusetts, Historical Society; Fredrick Lewis Weis, *Early Generations of the Family of Robert Harrington of Watertown, Massachusetts, 1634, and Some of His Descendants* (Worcester, Mass.: n.p., 1958); Benson J. Lossing, *Pictorial Field-Book of the Revolution* (New York: Harper and Brothers, 1852), CD Heritage Books, 2004, 1:554; "Great Celebration of the Battle of Concord," *(Massachusetts) Daily Atlas,* April 20, 1850, 2; "Funeral of Jonathan Harrington," *Sun,* April 1, 1854, 1; "Funeral of Jonathan Harrington," *Boston Evening Transcript,* March 31, 1854, 1; Craig's Daguerreian Registry, www.daguerreotype.com. Also consulted: 1850 U.S. Census, Middlesex County, Massachusetts, population schedule, Lexington, p. 196 (digital number), dwelling 197, family

236, Jonathan Harrington, digital image, www.ancestry.com, citing National Archives, microfilm publication M432, roll 325.

Conrad Heyer

[Conrad Heyer], daguerreotype, in the collections of the Maine Historical Society, image no. 13428; Church of Jesus Christ of Latter-day Saints [LDS], "Ancestral File," database, Conrad Heyer family group record, submitted by Harry McClean, www.familysearch.org; Wilford W. Whitaker and Gary T. Horlacher, *Broad Bay Pioneers* (Rockport, Maine: Picton Press, 1998); Samuel L. Miller, *History of the Town of Waldoboro, Maine* (Waldeboro, Maine: Emerson, 1910); Revolutionary War Pension File, Conrad Heyer, file no. S35, 457/28.520–160–55; "Mortuary Notice," *Farmer's Cabinet (New Hampshire),* March 13, 1856, 2; "A Veteran," *Boston Daily Evening Transcript,* November 13, 1852, 1.

Ebenezer Hubbard

[Ebenezer Hubbard], photographic print, September 6, 1870, in the collections of the Concord Free Library; "Ebenezer Hubbard, September 6, 1870, from a carte de visite (source unrecorded)," online catalog record, www.concordnet.org/library/scollect/Portrait_Exhibit.44.html (accessed July 15, 2005); Church of Jesus Christ of Latter-day Saints [LDS], "Ancestral File," database, Ebenezer Hubbard family group record, multiple submitters, www.familysearch.org; William Willis Hayward, *The History of Hancock, New Hampshire, 1764–1889* (Lowell, Mass.: Vox Populi Press, S. W. Huse and Co., 1889); Deborah Bier, "The Concord and Lexington Minuteman Statues," *Concord Magazine,* www.concordma.com/magazine/sept98/minman.html (accessed Jan. 24, 2008). Also consulted: Eva L. Moffatt, "The Ancestry of William Forbes of Barre, Mass., and Montreal, Que. 1778–1833," ed. and correlated by Geoffrey Gilbert, typescript, 1953.

Agrippa Hull

Unknown artist, portrait of Agrippa Hull, oil, 1848 (after daguerreotype by Anson Clark, 1844), Stockbridge Library Association, Stockbridge, Massachusetts; Anson Clark, "Agrippa Hull," daguerreotype, March 18, 1844, in the collection of the Stockbridge Library Association; Electa F. Jones, *Stockbridge, Past and Present; or, Records of an Old Mission Station* (Springfield: Samuel Bowles and Company, 1854); Emilie S. Piper, "The Family of Agrippa Hull," *Berkshire Genealogist* 22, no. 1 (2001): 3–6, and "The Family of Agrippa Hull: Notes and Sources," *Berkshire Genealogist* 22, no. 2 (2001): 53–55; Revolutionary War Pension Files, John Langdon, file no. W760/BLWT4326–100/BLWT32–60–55/BLWT 4326–100, www.footnote.com; Thomas Egleston, *The Life of John Patterson* (New York: Knickerbocker Press, 1894); Sarah Cabot Sedgwick and Christina Sedgwick Marquand, *Stockbridge, 1739–1939: A Chronicle* (Great Barrington, Mass.: Berkshire Courier, 1939); "A Good Example," *(Stockbridge, Mass.) Weekly Visitor,* March 25, 1841, transcription. Also consulted: *African American and American Indian Patriots of the Revolutionary War* (Washington, D.C.: National Daughters of the American Revolution, 2001); "Agrippa Hull Enlist," *Mass Moments,* www.massmoments.org/moment.cfm?mid=130 (accessed May 12, 2005); "Agrippa Hull testimonials," typescript, 1950 Ms S-535, located at the Massachusetts Historical Society; Sidney Kaplan and Emma Nogrady Kaplan, *The Black Presence in the Era of the American Revolution* (Amherst: Univ. of Massachusetts Press, 1989).

Margaret Timbrooke Hull

[Margaret Timbrooke Hull], carte de visite, c. 1868, located at the Stockbridge Library Association; Emilie S. Piper, "The Family of Agrippa Hull," *Berkshire Genealogist* 22, no. 1 (2001): 3–6, and "The Family of Agrippa Hull: Notes and Sources," *Berkshire Genealogist* 22, no. 2 (2001): 53–55; Sarah Cabot Sedgwick and Christina Sedgwick Marquand, *Stockbridge, 1739–1939: A Chronicle* (Great Barrington, Mass.: Berkshire Courier, 1939); Death notice, "Peggy Hull," *(Lee, Massachusetts) Gleaner and Advocate,* May 19, 1870, 2; "Stockbridge," *Pittsfield Sun,* May 26, 1870, 2.

William Hutchings

Reverend E. B. Hillard, *The Last Men of the Revolution* (1864; repr., Barre, Mass.: Barre, 1968); Revolutionary War Pension File, William Hutchings, file no. S22320/BLWT2022–160–55; [Bangor; William Hutchings; Penobscot], *Lowell Daily Citizen and News,* July 12, 1865, 2; "The Last Revolutionary Pensioner in New England, and the Last but one upon the Rolls," paper read before the Maine Historical Society on the 19th of February 1874 by Hon. Joseph Williamson, *American Historical Record,* ed. Benson J. Lossing (Philadelphia: John E. Potter, 1874). Also consulted: F. Lee Betz, *The Last New England Private Yankee Doodle* (Litchfield, Conn.: My Country Society, 2004); "The Last Men of the Revolution: William Hutchings," www.americanrevolution.org/lastmen5.html (accessed Jan. 25, 2005); James W. Richardson, "The Last Revolutionary," *Yankee,* July 1989, 28.

Andrew Jackson

Edward Anthony, photographer, "Andrew Jackson," [between 1844 and 1845], in the collections of the Library of Congress, Dag no. 110; T. Doney, engraver, "Andrew Jackson: His Last Days," in the collection of the Library of Congress, April 15, 1845; Robert V. Remini, *Andrew Jackson and the Course of American Empire, 1767–1821* (New York: Harper and Row, 1977); "Biographical Sketch of General Andrew Jackson," *Sun,* June 19, 1845, 1.

David Kinnison

"David Kinnison, aged 112 yrs," daguerreotype, n.d., in the collection of the Western Reserve Historical Society; Vivian Lyon Moore, "The Last Survivor: The Story of a Veteran of the Boston Tea Party," *National Historical Magazine* 74 (December 1940): 40–43, 94; Benson J. Lossing, *Pictorial Field-Book of the Revolution* (New York: Harper and Brothers, 1852), CD Heritage Books, 2004, 1:499–500; Revolutionary War Pension File, David Kinnison/Kinniston, file no. S42782/BLWT14607–160–1812; Benson J. Lossing, "The Boston Tea Party," in *Harper's New Monthly Magazine,* December 1851–May 1852, 1–11. Also consulted: "Name: David Kennison," *Revolutionary Soldiers Buried in Illinois,* n.p., 1917 digital image, www.ancestry.com; James Edgar Brown, "David Kennison, Patriot and Centenarian, Who 'Poured' at the Boston Tea Party," *Official Bulletin, National Society, S.A.R.*, n.d.; Sherry J. Cooper, "Descendants of Robert (Kiniston) Keniston," typescript, n.d.; "David Kennison and the Chicago Sting," typescript, accession number 173.159, located at the Daughters of the American Revolution Library, Washington, D.C.; e-mail from Ann Sindelar to Maureen Taylor, February 1, 2006; letter from Sherry J. Cooper to Maureen Taylor, August 1, 2005; "Uncle David and His Little Tea Party," July 3, 2007, http://simplymarvelous.wordpress.com/2007/07/03/uncle-david-and-his-little-tea-party/ (accessed Oct. 30, 2007); Harold Francis Pfister, *Facing the Light: Historic American Portrait Daguerreotypes* (Washington, D.C.: National Portrait Gallery by Smithsonian Institution Press, 1978); "The Boston Tea Party," *Ohio Statesman,* January 13, 1852, 4; Edward L. Pierce, "Recollections as a Source of History," *Proceedings of the Massachusetts Historical Society,* 2nd series, vol. 10 (1896): 473–91.

John Kitts

Norval H. Busey, "John Kitts," Baltimore, Maryland, "1869" [date written on reverse side of image], in the collection of Chester Urban; 1870 U.S. Census, Baltimore County, Maryland, population schedule, Baltimore, 9th Ward, p. 375 (stamped), dwelling 135, family 214, John Kitts, digital image, ProQuest, Heritage Quest Online, citing National Archives, microfilm M593, roll 575; Thomas Dring, *Recollections of the Jersey Prison Ship* (Morrisania, N.Y.: n.p., 1865); Revolutionary War Pension File, John Kitts, file no. R6001, www.footnote.com; "John Kitts; Baltimore; City; Council; Revolution," *New Hampshire Sentinel,* October 21, 1869, 2; "The Oldest Citizen: Visit of a Veteran to the President and Congress," *Georgia Weekly Telegraph,* February 22, 1870, 4; "John Kitts; Baltimore; Sunday," *New Hampshire Patriot,* September 21, 1870, 2.

Uzal Knapp
D. Esterly, "Uzal Knapp," 1847, daguerreotype, in the collection of the New-York Historical Society; "The Last of Washington's Life Guard: Death of Uzal Knapp," *Daily Ohio Statesman,* January 29, 1856, 1; Benson J. Lossing, *Pictorial Field-Book of the Revolution* (New York: Harper and Brothers, 1852), CD Heritage Books, 2004, 1:687–88; Revolutionary War Pension Files, Uzal Knapp, file no. S16182/BLWT6066–100, www.footnote.com. Also consulted: Margaret V. S. Wallace, "'Big' Little Britain Uzal Knapp," *Orange County Post,* July 6, 1967; digital image, www.ancestry.com.

John Langdon
"John Langdon," daguerreotype, 1845, William Lithgow Willey Papers, MSS C5477, R. Stanton Avery Special Collections Department, New England Historic Genealogical Society; Revolutionary War Pension Files, John Langdon, file no. S29960, www.footnote.com; e-mail from David Allen Lambert to Maureen Taylor, June 19, 2004; diary of John Langdon, Mss A 2049, R. Stanton Avery Special Collections Department, New England Historic Genealogical Society; "Deaths," *Daily Evening Transcript,* November 27, 1848, 2.

Enoch Leathers
Edgar Crosby Smith, "Sketches of Some Revolutionary Soldiers of Piscataquis County," in *Historical Collections of Piscataquis County, Maine* (Dover, Maine: Observer Press, 1910); Revolutionary War Pension Files, Enoch Leathers, file no. S37618/BLWT15437–160–12, www.footnote.com; John Francis Sprague, *Sangerville, Maine, 1814–1914: Proceeding of the Centennial Celebration, June 13, 1814* (Dover, Maine: n.p., 1914). Also consulted: Advertisement, *Bangor (Maine) Register,* September 19, 1822, 3.

Dr. Jonathan Leonard
[Jonathan Leonard], daguerreotype, n.d., in the collection of Jonathan A. Shaw; e-mail from Jonathan A. Shaw to Maureen Taylor, September 14, 2004; Jonathan A. Shaw, *Doctor Jonathan Leonard (1763–1849),* typescript, n.d.; Caroline Leonard Goodenough, *Legends, Loves, and Loyalties of Old New England* (Rochester, Mass.: Author, n.d.); Death notice, *Sandwich Observer,* January 27, 1849, 2; "Jonathan Leonard, M.D.," *Sandwich Observer,* February 3, 1849, 2.

Morgan Lewis
Francis D'Avignon, lithographer, 1825, "Morgan Lewis," lithograph after a daguerreotype by Howard J. Chilton, appeared in *Memoir, prepared at the request of a committee of the Common Council of the City of New York . . .* (1826), located in Print Collection, Miriam and Ira D. Wallach Division of Art, Prints and Photographs, Astor, Lenox and Tilden Foundations, New York Public Library; Revolutionary War Pension Files, Morgan Lewis, file no. S16447, www.footnote.com; Julia Livingston Delafield, *Biographies of Francis Lewis and Morgan Lewis* (New York: A. D. F. Randolph and Company, 1877). Also consulted: Lewis Herring and James B. Longacre, *The National Portrait Gallery of Distinguished Americans with Biographical Sketches* (Philadelphia: D. Rice and A. N. Hart, 1854); John A. Garraty and Mark C. Carnes, *American National Biography* (New York: Oxford Univ. Press, 1999), vol. 17, sv "Lewis, Morgan"; Michael Bellesile, "Lewis, Morgan," *Encyclopedia of the American Revolution,* Library of Military History, ed. Harold Selesky, vol. 1 (Detroit: Charles Scribner's Sons, 2006); *Gale Virtual Reference Library,* Thomson Gale, Boston Public Library (accessed July 3, 2007); Benson J. Lossing, *Pictorial Field-Book of the Revolution* (New York: Harper and Brothers, 1852), CD Heritage Books, 2004, 1:55, 270, 281; 1790 U.S. Census, Dutchess County, New York, Rhinebeck Township, p. 152, col. 2, line 28, Morgan Lewis, digital image, ProQuest, Heritage Quest Online, citing National Archives, microfilm M637, roll 6; 1800 U.S. Census, Dutchess County, New York, Clinton, p. 108 (penned upper left), line 16, Morgan Lewis, digital image, ProQuest, Heritage Quest Online, citing National Archives, microfilm M32,

roll 21; 1810 U.S. Census, Dutchess County, New York, Clinton, p. 207 (upper left corner), line 37, Morgan Lewis, digital image, ProQuest, Heritage Quest Online, citing National Archives, microfilm M252, roll 30; 1820 U.S. Census, Dutchess County, New York, Clinton, p. 33 (upper left corner), line 54, Morgan Lewis, digital image, ProQuest, Heritage Quest Online, citing National Archives, microfilm M33, roll 71.

ADAM LINK
Reverend E. B. Hillard, *The Last Men of the Revolution* (1864; repr., Barre, Mass.: Barre, 1968); Revolutionary War Pension Files, Adam Link, file no. S1771/BLWT26343-160-55, www.footnote.com.

DOLLEY (PAYNE) MADISON
"Dolley Madison," daguerreotype, c. 1840, in the collection of the Maine Historical Society, image no. 5520; Richard N. Côté, *Strength and Honor: The Life of Dolley Madison* (Mt. Pleasant, S.C.: Corinthian Books, 2004); Catherine Dean, "The History of Scotchtown," *Scotchtown: The House and the Plantation,* 2007, www.apva.org/scotchtown/house/ (accessed Oct. 27, 2007); "Dolley Madison," *Women in History,* 2007, www.lkwdpl.org/wihohio/madi-dol.htm (accessed July 17, 2007); Irving Brant, "Madison, Dolley Payne Todd," *Notable American Women* (Cambridge, Mass.: Belknap Press of Harvard University, 1971), vol. 2, sv "Building on History"; *Portland Press,* March 25, 2005; President James Polk and family (with future president James Buchanan, far left) on the South Portico, the woman to the president's left (head blurred) is former First Lady Dolley Madison, c. 1849, daguerreotype, in the collection of the George Eastman House, Rochester, New York.

JOHN MCCRILLIS
J. Parker, photographer, John McCrillis, card photograph, Newport, New Hampshire, c. 1870, collection of David Allen Lambert; Walter R. Nelson, *History of Goshen: New Hampshire* (n.p., 1957); Doris Nelson Newman and Harry W. Wasasier, *A Supplement to the History of Goshen, N.H.* (Goshen, N.H.: Goshen Historical Society, 1976).

ALEXANDER MILLINER/MARONEY
Reverend E. B. Hillard, *The Last Men of the Revolution* (1864; repr., Barre, Mass.: Barre, 1968); Revolutionary War Pension File, Alexander Maroney, file no. S42925/BLWT17708-160-55, www.footnote.com; "Mortuary Notice," *Milwaukee Daily Sentinel,* March 22, 1865, 2.

NIKONAH
Horatio Hale, "Nikonah," photographic print, 1870, in the collection of the American Philosophical Society; e-mail from Valerie-Ann Lutz to Maureen Taylor, January 19, 2006; Frederick Webb Hodge, *Handbook of American Indians North of Mexico* (Washington, D.C.: GPO, 1912); *Tutelo Indian Tribe History,* www.accessgenealogy.com (accessed Jan. 22, 2007); *Tutelo Tribe,* www.tutelotribe.com/ (accessed Oct. 10, 2009); Horatio Hale, "The Tutelo Tribe and Language Read before the American Philosophical Society," *Proceedings of the American Philosophical Society* 21, no. 114 (1883): 1–45; Benson J. Lossing, *Pictorial Field-Book of the Revolution* (New York: Harper and Brothers, 1852), CD Heritage Books, 2004, 1:247. Also consulted: Henry H. Mitchell, *The Pittsylvania Packet,* Pittsylvania Historical Society, Chatham, Virginia 1997 (Winter 1997): 4–8, digital image, available online at www.victorianvilla.com/sims-mitchell/local/native/redis.htm (accessed Feb. 7, 2007).

TIRZAH (WHITNEY) PALMER
"Grandmother Palmer," caption on daguerreotype, in the collection of Joseph Bauman; Letter from Joe Bauman to Maureen Taylor, September 18, 2005; Horace Wilbur Palmer, "Palmer in America," typescript, 1915–53, MSS 297, located at New England Historic Genealogical Society; Church of Jesus Christ of Latter-day Saints [LDS],

"Ancestral File," database, www.familysearch.org, Noah Palmer family group record, multiple submitters; Revolutionary War Pension Files, Widow's Pension, Noah Palmer, file no. R7904/BLWT45716-160-55, www.footnote.com. Also consulted: 1790 U.S. Census, Bennington County, Vermont, Manchester, p. 13 (penned upper right), col. 2, line 28, Noah Palmer, digital image, ProQuest, Heritage Quest Online, citing National Archives, microfilm M637, roll 13; 1800 U.S. Census, Washington County, New York, Kingsbury, p. 413 (penned bottom right), line 35, Noah Palmer, digital image, ProQuest, Heritage Quest Online, citing National Archives, microfilm M32, roll 26; 1810 U.S. Census, Chenango County, New York, Sherburne, p. 184 (upper left), p. 1081 (penned along right edge), line 42, Noah Palmer, digital image, ProQuest, Heritage Quest Online, citing National Archives, microfilm M252, roll 26; 1820 U.S. Census, Chenango County, New York, Sherburne, p. 183 (upper left), p. 342 (penned left margin), line 42, Noah Palmer, digital image, ProQuest, Heritage Quest Online, citing National Archives, microfilm M33, roll 66.

Thomas Handasyd Perkins

"Col. Thomas H. Perkins of Boston," daguerreotype, c. 1853, located at the Boston Athenaeum UTB-2 5.4 Per.t. (no. 1); John A. Garraty and Mark C. Carnes, *American National Biography* (New York: Oxford, Univ. Press, 1999), vol. 17, sv "Perkins, Thomas Handasyd"; Justin Winsor, ed., *The Memorial History of Boston, 1630–1880* (Boston: James R. Osgood and Company, 1881); "Unitarianism in America," www.harvardswuarelibrary.org/UIA%Online/perkinsth.html (accessed Feb. 2, 2006); Carl Seaburg and Stanley Patterson, *Merchant Prince of Boston* (Cambridge, Mass.: Harvard Univ. Press, 1971); Thomas G. Cary, *Memoir of T. H. Perkins* (n.p., 1856); "Death of Hon. Thomas Handasyd Perkins," *Farmer's Cabinet (New Hampshire),* January 9, 1854, 2; "Death of an old merchant," *(Maryland) Sun,* January 12, 1854, 2; Daniel Webster, *An Address Delivered at the Laying of the Cornerstone of the Bunker Hill Monument* (Boston: Cummings, Hillard and Company, 1825).

William Plumer

[William Plummer], daguerreotype, c. 1840–50, in the collections of the New Hampshire Historical Society; Lynn W. Turner, *William Plumer of New Hampshire, 1759–1850,* Institute of Early American History and Culture at Williamsburg, Virginia (Chapel Hill: Univ. of North Carolina Press, 1962); John A. Garraty and Mark C. Carnes, *American National Biography* (New York: Oxford Univ. Press, 1999), vol. 17, sv "Plumer, William"; "Plumer, William (1759–1850)," *Biographical Directory of the United States Congress,* www.bioguide.congress.gov/scripts/biodisplay.pl?index=P000393; "Death of Gov. Plumer," *New Hampshire Patriot and State Gazette,* January 2, 1851, 2; "Mortuary Notice," *Farmer's Cabinet (New Hampshire),* December 12, 1850, 2. Also consulted: 1800 U.S. Census, Rockingham County, New Hampshire, Epping, p. 715, line 10, "Wm. Plumer," digital image, ProQuest, Heritage Quest Online, citing National Archives, microfilm M32, roll 20; 1810 U.S. Census, Rockingham County, New Hampshire, Epping, p. 57 (upper right), p. 31 (penned upper right), p. 404 (penned right margin), line 20, William Plumer, digital image, ProQuest, Heritage Quest Online, citing National Archives, microfilm M252, roll 25; 1820 U.S. Census, Rockingham County, New Hampshire, Epping, p. 170 (upper left), line 6, William Plumer, digital image, ProQuest, Heritage Quest Online, citing National Archives, microfilm M33, roll 60; www.senate.gov/artandhistory/minute/Dear_Diary.htm; Everett Brown, ed., *William Plummer's Memorandum in the United States Senate 1803–1807* (1923; repr., New York: Da Capo Press, 1969).

Jeremiah Powell

[Jeremiah Powell], photographic print, n.d., in the collection of Richard Powell Draves; Richard Powell Draves, *Jeremiah Powell: A Short Biography,* typescript, 2004; Revolutionary War Pension File, Jeremiah Powell, file no. S11259, www.footnote.com.

Isaac Rice

Benson J. Lossing, *Pictorial Field-Book of the Revolution* (New York: Harper and Brothers, 1852), CD Heritage Books, 2004, 1:122; Mark M. Boatner III, *Encyclopedia of the American Revolution* (repr., Mechanicsburg, Pa.: Stackpole Books, 1994), entries for "St. Clair," "Arthur," and "Allen"; Death notice, *[Vermont] Semi-Weekly Eagle,* August 23, 1852, 3.

Chief Sopiel Selmore

"Chief Sopiel Selmore," photographic print, c. 1900, in the collection of the Maine Historical Society, Photographs-OS-People-S, 2002.500.043; Mark M. Boatner III, *Encyclopedia of the American Revolution* (repr., Mechanicsburg, Pa.: Stackpole Books, 1994), entry for "Indians in the Colonial Wars and in the Revolution"; Sharon Malinowski, *Gale Encyclopedia of Native American Tribes* (Detroit: Gale Research International, 1998), entry for "Passamaquoddy"; Application for membership for Sopiel Selmore, Maine Society of the Sons of the American Revolution, January 29, 1805, national no. 6508; "Register of Actual Sons of Soldiers, Sailors, and Recognized Patriots of the War of the Revolution Who Have Been Enrolled as Members of the National Society of the Sons of the American Revolution, April 30, 1889, to July 1, 1908," in *National Year Book, 1908,* comp. Clark A. Howard (n.p.: National Society of the Sons of the American Revolution, n.d.); 1900 U.S. Census, Washington County, Maine, population schedule, Perry Town, p. 364 (stamped), dwelling 230, family 237, Sopiel Selmore, digital image, ProQuest, Heritage Quest Online, citing National Archives, Microfilm T623, roll 602; "Building on History," *Portland Press,* September 7, 1996. Also consulted: David L. Ghere, "Passamaquoddy/Penobscot," *Encyclopedia of North American Indians,* www.college.hmco.com/history/readerscomp/naind/html/na_028100_passamaquodd.htm (accessed May 11, 2005).

Six Aged Citizens of Bennington

"Six Aged Citizens of Benington," daguerreotype, 1848, located at Bennington Museum, image no. A901; "From the Family Bible Owned by Landlord Stephen Fay of the Catamount Tavern," www.freepages.genealogy.rootsweb.com/~fayfamily/biblepage10.html (accessed Oct. 27, 2007); Samuel Fay, daguerreotype, in the collections of the Bennington Museum, Bennington, Vermont, image no. A2888; Isaac Jennings, *Memorials of a Century: Embracing a Record of Individuals and Events Chiefly in the Early History of Bennington, V.T., and Its First Church* (Boston: Gould and Lincoln, 1869); "Bennington Battle," *Vermont Gazette,* August 21, 1840; "The Catamount Tavern," Bennington Area Chamber of Commerce and the Town of Bennington, www.bennington.com/chamber/walking/catamount descrip.html (accessed Oct. 27, 2007).

(Possibly) David Smiley

[David Smiley], five daguerreotypes in the collection of William L. Schaeffer; e-mail from William L. Schaeffer to Maureen Taylor, January 18, 2006; Revolutionary War Pension Files, David Smiley, file no. S43164/BLWT5216–160–55, www.footnote.com; Albert Smith, *History of the Town of Peterborough, Hillsborough County New Hampshire . . .* (Boston: Press of G. H. Ellis, 1876); "Mortuary Notice," *New-Hampshire Sentinel,* October 26, 1855, 3.

Isaac Snow

[Isaac Snow], photographic print, copy from a daguerreotype, in the collection of the Orleans Historical Society, Massachusetts; e-mail from Tamsen Cornell to Maureen Taylor, March 11, 2008; William Richard Cutter, *Historic Homes and Places and Genealogical and Personal Memoirs,* 2 vols. (New York: Lewis Historical, 1908); Revolutionary War Pension Files, Isaac Snow, file no. S19098, www.footnote.com; Louis F. Middlebrook, *Exploits of the Connecticut Ship "Defence," Commanded by Captain Samuel Smedley of Fairfield, Connecticut, Revolutionary War* (Hartford,

Conn.: n.p., 1922), digital image, available online at www.world vitalrecords.com/indexinfo.aspx?ix=godfrey_exploitsofthe connecticutship1922.

Clark Stevens

Southworth and Hawes, attribution, [portrait of Clark Stevens], Boston Athenaeum, 1850, call number UTB-2 5.4 Ste., c. 1850; anonymous, *Mattapoisett and old Rochester, Massachusetts: Being a history of these towns and also in part of Marion and a portion of Wareham* (New York: Grafton Press, 1907); Margery S. Walker, *Early Friends in East Montpelier* (n.p.: OMlet Publications, 2000), www.Plainfieldfriends.tripod.com/VT/walker.htm (accessed Feb. 2, 2006); D. P. Thompson, *History of the Town of Montpelier from the Time It Was First Chartered in 1781 to the Year 1860. Together with Biographical Sketches of Its Most Noted Deceased Citizens* (Montpelier, Vt.: E. P. Walton, 1860).

Flora Stewart

"Mrs. Flora Stewart," card photograph, Manchester, New Hampshire, November 5, 1867, collection of Greg French; "Mrs. Flora Stewart; New Hampshire; Londonderry," *Farmer's Cabinet (New Hampshire),* August 27, 1868, 2; "The Oldest Person in New Hampshire," *Farmer's Cabinet (New Hampshire),* May 23, 1867, 2; "Flora Stuart," *Farmer's Cabinet (New Hampshire),* June 27, 1867, 2; "The Oldest Person Known," *New England Historical Genealogical Register* 22 (July 1868): 310; Bailey Moore, *History of the Town of Candia, Rockingham County, N.H., from Its First Settlement to the Present Time* (Manchester, N.H.: George W. Browne, 1893); Douglas Harper, *Slavery in New Hampshire,* 2003, www.slavenorth .com/newhampshire.htm (accessed Nov. 14, 2007); Daniel Gage Annis, comp., *Vital Records of Londonderry, New Hampshire* (Manchester, N.H.: Granite State, 1914; repr., Baltimore: Genealogical Publishing, 1994); "An Old Lady," *Lowell Daily Citizen and News,* November 8, 1867, 2.

Jabez Huntington Tomlinson

Daguerreotypist unknown, "Jabez Huntington Tomlinson (1760–1849)," daguerreotype in the collection of Yale University Art Gallery, image no. 1942.110, gift of Mrs. Thomas L. Ellis and Mrs. James Pederson; Henry P. Johnston, *Yale and Her Honor-Roll in the American Revolution 1775–1783* (New York: Privately printed, 1888); Louise Pearsons Dolliver, *Lineage Book National Society of the Daughters of the American Revolution* (Washington, D.C.: n.p., 1898); William Howard Wilcoxson, *History of Stratford, Connecticut: 1639–1939* (Stratford, Conn.: Stratford Tercentenary Commission, 1939); Bruce P. Stark, *Guide to the Tomlinson Family Papers,* manuscript group 1172, Yale University, May 1982; Revolutionary War Pension File, Widow's Pension, Jabez H. Tomlinson/Phebe Tomlinson, file no. W6305, www.footnote.com.

Mary Hunt Palmer Tyler

"Mary Tyler," daguerreotype, c. 1860, in the collection of the Vermont Historical Society; Revolutionary War Pension Files, Widow's Pension, file no. S29850, www.footnote.com; Mary Palmer Tyler, *Grandmother Tyler's Book* (New York: Knickerbocker Press, 1925); "Mary Tyler," in *Glimpses of the Human Experience from the Vermont Historical Society Collections* (Barre: Vermont Historical Society, undated brochure); Paul P. Reuben, "Royall Tyler," chap. 8 in *PAL: Perspectives in American Literature; A Research and Reference Guide—An Ongoing Project,* www.web.csustan.edu/English/ reuben/pal/chap8/tyler.html (accessed Dec. 13, 2007); Mary Palmer Tyler, *The Maternal Physician: A Treatise in the Nature and Management of Infants* (n.p., 1818). Also consulted: Henry Burnham, *Brattleboro, Windham County, Vermont: Early History with Biographical Sketches of Some of Its Citizens* (Brattleboro, Vt.: D. Leonard, 1880); "Gen. John Steele Tyler," in *The New England Historical and Genealogical Register,* online database, www.new englandancestors.org, New England Historic Genealogical Society, 2001–7, orig. pub. as New England Historic Genealogical

Society, *The New England Historical and Genealogical Register,* 158 vols. (1847–2004): 1876:243.

Nicholas G. Veeder

"Nicholas Veeder," photographic print, c. 1860, in the collection of the Schenectady Historical Society, New York; Vreeland Y. Leonard, "The Genealogical Record of the Veeder Family," typescript, 1937; Revolutionary War Pension Files, Nicholas Veeder, file no. S16283/BLWT8448–160–55, www.footnote.com; "Nicholas G. Veeder, Ex-Revolutionary Soldier," National Society Daughters of the American Revolution, http://members.aol.com/B1093/myhomepage/soldier.htm (accessed Aug. 6, 2004); "Nicholas Veeder," University of the State of New York/New York State Education Department, www.nysm.nysed.gov/research_collections/research/history/three/bat7.html (accessed Jan. 25, 2005).

Nathan Walden Jr.

[Nathan Walden], photographic print, n.d., in the collection of Crane C. Walden; e-mail from Crane Walden to Maureen Taylor, November 19, 2003; Revolutionary War Pension Files, Nathan Walden, file no. S43234, www.footnote.com; *U.S. Pensioners, 1818–1872* [database online, www.ancestry.com], Provo, Utah, Generations Network, 2007, original data from Ledgers of Payments, 1818–72, to U.S. Pensioners under Acts of 1818 through 1858 from Records of the Office of the Third Auditor of the Treasury, 1818–72, National Archives, microfilm T718, 23 rolls, Records of the Accounting Officers of the Department of the Treasury, RG 217, National Archives, Washington, D.C. (accessed Oct. 15, 2009).

Daniel Waldo

Churchill and Denison, "Daniel Waldo," card photograph, Albany, New York, c. 1860, collection of David Allen Lambert; Reverend E. B. Hillard, *The Last Men of the Revolution* (1864; repr., Barre, Mass.: Barre, 1968); Revolutionary War Pension Files, Daniel Waldo, file no. S14782/BLWT28501–160–55, www.footnote.com; Franklin Bowditch Dexter, *Biographical Sketches of the Graduates of Yale College with Annals of the College History* (New York: Henry Holt and Company, 1907); "Death of Father Waldo," *(Maryland) Sun,* August 4, 1864, 4; "Accident," *(Maryland) Sun,* July 15, 1864, 2; "Death of Father Waldo," *Philadelphia Inquirer,* August 3, 1864, 8; Waldo A. B. Lincoln, *Genealogy of the Waldo Family: A Record of the Descendants of Cornelius Waldo of Ipswich, Mass, from 1647 to 1900* (Worcester, Mass.: Press of Charles Hamilton, 1902).

Abraham Wheelwright

Captain William H. Bayley and Captain Oliver O. Jones, *History of the Marine Society of Newburyport, Massachusetts . . .* (Newburyport, Mass.: Daily News Press, 1906); Revolutionary War Pension Files, Abraham Wheelwright, file no. S19158, www.footnote.com.

John Williams

Stephen A. Dexter, [John Williams], carte de visite, c. 1871, in the collection of Theresa Franks; "Died," *Providence Journal,* October 16, 1874, 2; Sydney James, *Colonial Rhode Island: A History* (New York: Charles Scribner's Sons, 1975); Kenneth S. Carlson, "Rhode Island General Assembly—Slavery Related Legislation," typescript, Rhode Island State Archives, n.d.; 1850 U.S. Census, Providence County, Rhode Island, population schedule, Providence, ward 1, p. 59 (penned in upper right), p. 30 (stamped), dwelling 372, family 527, John Williams, digital image, www.ancestry.com, citing National Archives, microfilm M432, roll 844; 1860 U.S. Census, Providence County, Rhode Island, population schedule, Providence, ward 1, p. 26 (penned), dwelling 142, family 200, John Williams, digital image, www.ancestry.com, citing National Archives, microfilm M653, roll 1209; 1870 U.S. Census, Providence County, Rhode Island, population schedule, Providence, ward 1, p. 76 (penned upper left), dwelling 441, family 683, John Williams, digital image, www.ancestry.com, citing National Archives, microfilm M593, roll 1478.

Huldah Welles Wolcott

Augustus Washington, daguerreotypist, "Huldah Welles Wolcott," c. 1850, located at Connecticut Historical Society, image no. 1964.118.7; "Huldah Welles Wolcott (1760–1860)," 2005, www.npg.si.edu/exh/awash/huldah.htm (accessed Sept. 20, 2005); Revolutionary War Pension File, William Wolcott, Widow's Pension, file no. W26,090/BLWT11,070–160–55.

Joseph Wood Jr.

[Joseph Wood], photographic print, n.d., in the collection of Sandra MacLean Clunies; Sandra MacLean Clunies, "Joseph Wood Jr., 1759–1859," typescript, n.d.; Revolutionary War Pension File, Joseph Wood, file no. S17209/BLWT9051–160–55; Rev. Charles A. Downs, *History of Lebanon, N.H., 1761–1887* (Concord, N.H.: Rumford, 1908); "Veteran Graduates," *Farmer's Cabinet (New Hampshire),* August 12, 1857, 2; Ezra S. Stearns, comp., *Genealogical and Family History of the State of New Hampshire,* vol. 1 (New York: Lewis, 1908); A. B. Rich, *An Historical Discourse, Delivered at the Twenty-fifth Anniversary of the West Lebanon Congregational Church and Society, November 8, 1874* (Concord, N.H.: Republican Press Association, 1874); Sandra MacLean Clunies, "Joseph Wood's Will," transcription, n.d.; "Death Notice," *Farmer's Cabinet (New Hampshire),* January 11, 1860, 3.

Sarah "Sally" Sayward Barrell Keating Wood

[Sally Sayward Barrell Keating Wood (1759–1855)], probably Portland, Maine, c. 1845, daguerreotype, in the Maine Women Writers Collection, Westbrook College, Portland, Maine; Laurel Thatcher Ulrich, "'From the Fair to the Brave': Spheres of Womanhood in Federal Maine," in *Agreeable Situations: Society, Commerce, and Art in Southern Maine, 1780–1830,* ed. Laura Fecych Sprague (Kennebunk, Maine: Brick Store Museum, 1987); John A. Garraty and Mark C. Carnes. *American National Biography* (New York: Oxford Univ. Press, 1999), vol. 23, sv "Wood, Sally Sayward Barrell Keating"; Pat Higgins, "The Other Tea Party at York, Maine," www.imaginemaine.com/mainestories/Tea.html (accessed Oct. 27, 2007); "Death of an American Authoress," *(Maryland) Sun,* January 16, 1855, 4. Also consulted: 1850 U.S. Census, Oxford County, Maine, population census, Hartford, p. 28 (penned upper left), dwelling 193, family 212, Charles Wood, digital image, www.ancestry.com, citing National Archives, microfilm M432, roll 263.

Writing a book of biographical sketches is no simple task. The citations for each short biography do not cover the extensive research completed to both understand the time period or delve into the lives of the individuals. In addition to conducting historiographical studies of the era, I investigated all facets of everyday life. Of particular use was Dorothy Denneen Volo and James M. Volo, *Daily Life during the American Revolution* (Westport, Conn.: Greenwood Press, 2003); and Randall Huff, *The Revolutionary War Era* (Westport, Conn.: Greenwood Press, 2004).

A bibliographic study of the American Revolution could easily fill a volume. Obviously, this short bibliographic essay doesn't begin to cover the breadth and depth of the literature—encompassing scholarly, mass-market, and digital collections. There are books and Web sites that are more comprehensive than this discussion. For instance, the extensive online bibliography prepared by the Omohundro Institute of Early American History and Culture covers published volumes and select articles from the *William and Mary Quarterly* (http://revolution.h-net.msu.edu/bib.html) and is a wonderful resource. A more focused approach is by Eric G. Grundset, library director at the National Society of the Daughters of the American Revolution Library. His *Forgotten Patriots: African American and American Indian Patriots in the Revolutionary War; A Guide to Service, Sources and Studies* (Washington, D.C.: National Society Daughters of the American Revolution, 2008) surveys material relating to two understudied groups that participated in the American Revolution. Another online resource is the American Revolution Web site (www.americanrevolution.org), which presents essays written on specific topics and includes links for historical information, genealogical research, and resources for reenactors.

BIBLIOGRAPHIC ESSAY

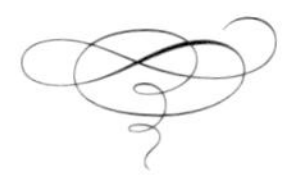

Reference Works

A series of library reference works were invaluable for fact checking or for adding minor details. Thomas L. Purvis, *Revolutionary America, 1763–1800* (New York: Facts on File, 1995), is full of charts and statistics that cover everything from schooling to famines and epidemics. Encyclopedias such as Gregory Fremont-Barnes, Richard Alan Ryerson, vol. eds., *American Revolutionary War: A Student Encyclopedia* (Santa Barbara, Calif.: ABC Clio, 2007); Paul Finkleman, ed., *Encyclopedia of the New American Nation: The Emergence of the United States, 1754–1829* (Detroit: Thompson/Gale, 2006); Harv Hilowitz, *The Revolutionary War Chronology and Almanac, 1754–1783: The Significant Events Leading to the Revolutionary War through to the Aftermath* (Saugerties, N.Y.: Hope Farm Press, 1995); and Mark M. Boatner, *Encyclopedia of the American Revolution* (Mechanicsburg, Pa.: Stackpole Books, 1994), were useful for quick background on major figures and battles.

Photographs

Image history along with specialized reading in the history of photography was necessary to explore the role of these images in keeping the memory of the Revolution alive with successive generations. David Hackett Fischer's fascinating book on the iconographic images of American history, *Liberty and Freedom: A Visual History of America's Founding Ideas* (New York: Oxford University Press, 2005), made me think about the photographs of the Revolutionary War generation as being iconographic representations of a "lost generation." For readers interested in learning more about processes presented in these images—daguerreotypes, tintypes, and card photographs—the following are useful references, as they cover the beginnings of photography in this country: Beaumont Newhall's classic *The Daguerreotype in America* (New York: Dover, 1976); Floyd Rinhart and Marion Rinhart, *The American Daguerreotype* (Athens: University of Georgia Press, 1981); and John Wood, ed., *America and the Daguerreotype* (Iowa City: University of Iowa Press, 1991). William Darrah, *Cartes de Visite in Nineteenth Century Photography* (Gettysburg, Pa.: William Darrah, 1981), is the best resource for early card photos. Tintypes are covered in Floyd Rinhart, Marion Rinhart, and Robert W. Wagner, *The American Tintype* (Columbus: Ohio State University Press, 1999); Steven Kasher, *America and the Tintype* (New York: ICP/Steidl, 2008); and Stanley B. Burns, *Forgotten Marriage: The Painted Tintype and the Decorative Frame, 1860–1910* (New York: Burns Press, 1995). For a general overview of the development of photography in this country, consult Keith F. Davis, *The Origins of American Photography, 1839–1885: From Daguerreotype to Dry-Plate* (New Haven, Conn.: Hall Family Foundation, in association with the Nelson-Atkins Museum of Art, 2007). Specific questions about processes or persons involved in early photography can be answered by the *Encyclopedia of Nineteenth-Century Photography*, ed. John Hannavy, 2 vols. (New York: Routledge, 2008). An excellent resource for daguerreotypists is *Craig's Daguerrian Registry* by John S. Craig, http://craigcamera.com/dag. While not current (it hasn't been updated since 1988), it contains details on thousands of daguerreotypists.

Costume

Studying the elements of a picture, such as the clothing worn, meant studying costume history. Invaluable were Joan Severa, *Dressed for the Photographer: Ordinary Americans and Fashion, 1840–1900* (Kent, Ohio: Kent State University Press, 1995); Severa, *My Likeness Taken: Daguerreian Portraits in America* (Kent, Ohio: Kent State University Press, 2005); John Peacock, *Men's Fashions* (London: Thames and Hudson, 1996); and Marian I. Doyle, *An Illustrated History of Hairstyles, 1830–1930* (Atglen, Pa.: Schiffer, 2003). For military uniforms, helpful volumes were Don Troiani,

Don Troiani's Soldiers of the American Revolution (Mechanicsburg, Pa.: Stackpole Books, 2007); Kevin F. Kiley, *An Illustrated Encyclopedia of Uniforms from 1775–1783: The American Revolutionary War* (London: Lorenz Books, 2008); and Kurt Stein, *Canes and Walking Sticks* (York, Pa.: Liberty Cap Books, 1974).

Background Reading

There is no shortage of material written about the Revolutionary period. Some are treatises like the award-winning Gordon S. Wood, *The Radicalism of the American Revolution* (New York: Vintage Books, 1991), or David McCullough's absorbing *1776* (New York: Simon and Schuster, 2006), a book that turns historical characters into living men and women. An interesting read was Ray Raphael, *A People's History of the American Revolution: How Common People Shaped the Fight for Independence* (New York: Perennial, 2001). Wood's recent *Revolutionary Characters: What Made the Founders Different* (New York: Penguin Press, 2006), and Joseph Ellis, *Founding Brothers: The Revolutionary War Generation* (New York: Vintage Press, 2002), offer insights into the men who worked to form this nation. The "founding mothers" are covered in Cokie Roberts, *Founding Mothers: The Women Who Raised Our Nation* (New York: William Morrow, 2004); Mary Beth Norton, *Liberty's Daughters: The Revolutionary Experience of American Women, 1750–1800* (Boston: Little, Brown and Co., 1980); and Carol Berkin, *Revolutionary Mothers: Women in the Struggle for America's Independence* (New York: Alfred Knopf, 2005). Eleanor Ellet's biographies in *The Women of the American Revolution* (1849; repr., Nashville: American History Imprints, 2004) promoted women's roles in the conflict in the nineteenth century. Edwin G. Burrows, *Forgotten Patriots: The Untold Story of American Prisoners during the Revolutionary War* (New York: Basic Books, 2008), explores the experiences of those men imprisoned during their service.

Compiled Lists

Lists of Revolutionary War soldiers appear in the *DAR Patriot Index,* compiled by the National Society of the Daughters of the American Revolution, 3 vols. (Washington, D.C.: National Society, Daughters of the American Revolution, 2003), and in *A Census of Pensioners for Revolutionary or Military Services,* prepared by the Genealogical Society of the Church of Jesus Christ of Latter-day Saints (Baltimore: Genealogical, 1965), which is based on material collected in the sixth United States census. Abstracts of pension records appear in Virgil D. White, *Genealogical Abstracts of Revolutionary War Pension Files,* 8 vols. (Waynesboro, Tenn.: National Historical, 1990, 1992). Francis B. Heiman, *Historical Register of Officers of the Continental Army during the War of the Revolution* (repr., Baltimore: Clearfield, 1997), provides the full names of the men mentioned in pension applications only by regiment name or surname. Patricia Law Hatcher, *Abstract of Graves of Revolutionary Patriots* (Westminster, Md.: Heritage Books, 2007), is based on information originally compiled and published in the Daughters of the American Revolution annual reports to the Smithsonian Institution issued from 1900 to 1974.

Primary Source Documents

In each short biography, I tried to let the men and women speak for themselves, which meant locating, as much as possible, material written by them. Access to primary source materials such as census records and pension applications is possible via subscription databases such as Ancestry.com or Footnote.com. For instance, census enumerations when available (not all of the men and women listed here appear in the census) provide a decade by decade insight into their household beginning with the first federal census of 1790. Only head of household names followed by statistics for that listing exist until the 1850 census. That's when the census begins including information such as names, ages, and birthplaces of individuals living within a household. Digitized census documents are available through Ancestry.com (individual subscription). Kathleen W. Hinckley, *Your Guide to the Federal Census for Genealogists, Researchers, and Family Historians* (Cincinnati: Betterway Books, 2002), is a good guide to what's available in census records.

Revolutionary War pension records contain documents written by soldiers, their widows, other family members, or friends. They are fascinating first-person accounts of an individual's activities both during the war and—often—afterward. Anyone interested in peeking into the everyday lives of their Revolutionary War ancestors should start by reading their pension files (if they applied for one) and then study the wider history of the period to place this information in a historical context. Complete pension documents are available through Footnote.com (individual subscription). Often the only mention of a woman's life appeared in the pension files.

For information on a soldier's life, from the end of his military service to his death, it was necessary to consult local histories and to read contemporary newspapers. Older published local histories are searchable through sources such as Ancestry.com and through searching Google.com's digital books library at www.books.google.com.

Newspapers are increasingly accessible via online collections available through GenealogyBank.com (individual subscription), Readex's Early American Newspapers (available through libraries), and Ancestry.com. You can read accounts from the pension office; view obituaries for the members of the Revolutionary generation, many of whom never sat for a picture (or for whom a picture couldn't be found); or just follow the stories of the day. It is necessary to bear in mind that the online newspaper archives are not comprehensive; however, there are still caches of newspapers available on the local level in libraries, archives, and historical societies. The National Endowment for the Humanities has sponsored grants for a United States Newspaper Program, which helps to preserve these resources. A list of participants by state is available on their Web site (www.neh.gov/projects/usnp.html).

While digitized documents are available online, treasure troves of original documents relating to the Revolutionary War are in the collections of the National Archives and in state and local historical societies. A good resource is James C. Neagles, *U.S. Military Records: A Guide to Federal and State Sources* (Salt Lake City, Utah: Ancestry, 1994). The National Archives has a partnership with Footnote.com and Ancestry.com to digitize materials. For instance, a database on Ancestry.com, called Revolutionary War Service Records, 1775–1783, actually contains material from the National Archives microfilm publication M246, *Revolutionary War Records, 1775–1783*, an index to muster rolls that contain name, rank, and unit. Thankfully, many of these organizations have Web sites with online catalogs and helpful reference staff. To locate manuscript material on specific individuals, contact the local historical society in the town in which they lived and the one from which they served, then contact the state historical society listed in American Association for State and Local History, *Directory of Historical Organizations in the United States and Canada*, 15th ed. (New York: Altamira, 2001), or use an online search engine to locate organizations and collections in your area.

Another option is to search for specific documents using the Library of Congress's National Union Catalog of Manuscript Collections (NUCMC, found at www.loc.gov/coll/nucmc/). This resource lets you find manuscript collections at libraries and other repositories. The NUCMC program began in 1959. Manuscript listings are in printed volumes only from 1959 to 1986, but information from 1986 to 1993 is available in both printed volumes and online through NUCMC. After 1993, the catalog is only online. Before you start searching, look under the information for researchers and read the page titled "Questions on Searching." The printed volumes of NUCMC are available in larger libraries. If your public library subscribes to ProQuest's Archives USA database, everything from 1959 to the present is searchable there.

Popular Media

The American Revolution is a popular topic for contemporary movies, both fictional and documentary. David McCullough's *John Adams* (2008, 501 minutes, HBO) lets viewers step into the life of a Founding Father, the PBS series *Liberty! The American Revolution* (2004, 360 minutes, PBS), and of course *The Patriot* (2000, 165 minutes, Sony Pictures) are dramatized versions of this period. There is an online discography of American Revolution movies on the Patriot Resource Web site (www.patriotresource.com/amerrev/index.html).